Cabin Cooking

Cabin Cooking

Rustic Cast Iron and Dutch Oven Recipes

COLLEEN SLOAN

GIBBS SMITH
TO ENRICH AND INSPIRE HUMANKIND

First Edition

16 15 14 13 12   5 4 3 2 1

Text © 2012 Colleen Sloan

Published by
Gibbs Smith
P.O. Box 667
Layton, Utah 84041

1.800.835.4993 orders
www.gibbs-smith.com

Designed by Kurt Wahlner
Printed and bound in Korea

Gibbs Smith books are printed on
either recycled, 100% post-consumer
waste, FSC-certified papers or on paper
produced from sustainable PEFC-
certified forest/controlled wood source.
Learn more at www.pefc.org.

This book is dedicated to my love of cooking in the out-of-doors and all those friendly cooks who have crossed my path or traveled with me.

Library of Congress Cataloging-in-Publication Data

Sloan, Colleen.
  Cabin cooking: rustic cast iron and dutch oven recipes / Colleen Sloan. —
1st ed.
      p. cm.
  Includes index.
  ISBN 978-1-4236-2247-5
1. Cooking, American. 2. Cookbooks. I. Title.
  TX715.S6367 2012
  641.5973—dc23
                          2011032742

Contents

Acknowledgments

Let me introduce myself to all who pick up and read this book. As of now, I am 73 years young and love every minute I can spend with all my Dutch oven cooking buddies and every cooking enthusiast I encounter. My dream was to share and gather knowledge from everyone I met. I've done that through cooking. I have no way of naming everyone who has contributed to the knowledge I can now share with others, but most know who you are. We all touch lives that we never know about—hopefully passing on your knowledge and sharing it with others is a part of your life. The history and recipes I've gathered are part of what I share, and so are my memories.

My children, Lisa, Steven, Larry (passed away in 1990), Justin, and Dustin, and my grandchildren and great-grandchildren are my taste testers. They also encourage me to keep going and creating. Cooking for camping trips, reunions, the Pony Express Reenactment, the Lewis and Clark Celebration, the Olympics, the IDOS organization, the Griswold and Cast Iron Collectors Society, fishing and hunting shows, company parties, birthdays, weddings, teaching classes, and demo's are just a small part of what I am privileged to do. God gave me a multitude of friends and acquaintances to share with—I'm sure you all know who you are and I thank you. God bless all of you for being in my life.

Remember to keep those pots hot and your buns warm. I'll see you on the trail or cross your path somewhere. And, like Mom used to say, "If it don't taste right, you probably left out the love."

HUGS, Colleen

The Log Cabin Lady

Introduction

Icons

Next to each recipe title are icons that show the various cooking methods that can be used to prepare the food. The below list identifies the icons you will see.

Dutch Oven   Cast Iron Skillet   Kitchen Oven   Kitchen Stove Top   Camp Stove   Slow Cooker   Volcano   Barbecue   Coals

Cooking Dutch

If ever the Old West comes to mind, just pull out the black pot and hang it over the campfire on a tripod. Smell the smoke of a thousand campfires and picture the pioneer women preparing a one-pot supper after a long day's walk. Hear the cowboys humming a tune as they wait for the camp cook to holler, "Come and get it. Lid's off!" The smells of a pot of beans and Dutch oven bread make your mouth water. The name "Dutch oven" is used quite loosely. It actually applies to any cast iron pot with a lid on it. The bottom is flat and it may or may not have legs. My first pot did not have legs, but now, most of them do.

Seasoning Your Dutch Oven

You just bought your first Dutch oven and now you're gonna take it home. As you're leaving the store, the salesperson tells you to be sure to season it before you use it. "Oh boy," you're thinking. "What does that mean?"

If you ask 100 people how to season a Dutch oven, you'll probably get 15 different answers. Most Dutch ovens today are coated with a protective substance by the manufacturer and all you need do is scrub it in hot soapy water, rinse it thoroughly with warm water, put it on the stove and heat it to over 212 degrees to thoroughly dry it. Let it cool then lightly grease it. Never use margarine or butter to season your pot. The lowest burning oils are bacon grease, lard, vegetable oil, or shortening. I love the taste of bacon, so I use a real light coat of bacon grease when it is available.

The next step is to take it outdoors and burn the oil into the metal pot at about 500 degrees. You can do this on your propane camp stove or on your volcano outdoor stove using 30 coals.

DO NOT DO THIS IN YOUR HOUSE OVEN!

All this does is bake a protective grease coating into the pot and virtually give your pot a no-scrub surface. If the pot appears to be sticky, you need to put it back on the heat and continue to burn the oil into the metal until you have a black carbon patina finish. If your heat is around medium-low on an outdoor propane stove, it should take less than an hour to cure or season a 12-inch Dutch oven. I always turn my Dutch ovens upside down so no grease will puddle in the bottom.

Cleaning Your Oven

If your pot is seasoned well and used often, you will find it very easy to clean. I always clean my pots while hot because it eases the release of the food particles. I find it helpful to return the pot to the heat after emptying it and spray it with a little vinegar water to soften the food. I use a solution of 1 part vinegar to 4 parts water and keep it in a spray bottle in my food box so I will have it everywhere I go. Vinegar is a great disinfectant and it will remove the excess grease and stop the build-up of oil in your pot.

A lot of people will tell you never to wash the inside of your pot with soap, but I have found on occasion that I have had to. I have a pot of my dad's that is over 50 years old and it has been washed several times. It has no legs and still cooks as good today as do any of my brand new ones. When you wash a cast iron pot, use only a mild detergent and always rinse it thoroughly with hot water to release the soap from the seasoning.

Always heat your pot on the stove or campfire after cleaning to dry out the moisture before storing it. It is not necessary to grease your oven before putting it away, but if you do, be sure to wipe it out thoroughly with a paper towel to avoid rancid oil build-up. Store your pots in a dry place with a clean paper towel inside to keep the moisture from rusting the surface.

These pots are not fragile, but they still require a certain amount of care. Dropping them or banging them against a hard surface could crack them and then their ability to hold the hot moisture that cooks your food is gone. You take care of them and they'll do you proud.

Using Your Dutch Oven

When using your Dutch oven for baking, the heat must be distributed on the top and bottom to maintain the proper temperature. Usually a 325–350 degree temperature is sufficient to bake almost any dish. If you are outside in the wind, it will take away some of your heat, but the following chart should help. You can raise or lower the temperature by adding 1 coal for every 18–20 degrees you wish to adjust the cooking temperature.

Oven Size	8"	10"	12"	14"	16"	22"
Top Coals (oven size + 3)	11	13	15	17	19	25

Oven Size	8"	10"	12"	14"	16"	22"
Bottom Coals (oven size -2)	6	8	10	12	14	20

Arranging the coals so that the heat remains even is also very important. Evenly place your coals in a circle underneath and on top of the Dutch oven. Never place coals in the middle underneath. Baking can be a lot of fun in a Dutch oven but proper heat is important. Always use more heat on top than on the bottom when cooking with coals.

If you are using a volcano or a collapsible stove, 12 coals with no top heat will keep your oven at 350–375 degrees. Use the damper (control ring) to control the burning rate.

Use a good name brand of coals for a more even heat. Coals are a great storage fuel because they don't evaporate or turn into gel.

The recipes in this cookbook will provide additional information to help you achieve Dutch oven and cast iron cooking success!

Breads

Dry Baking Mix

2 cups flour

1 tablespoon sugar

1 tablespoon baking powder

$1/2$ teaspoon salt

$1/2$ cup powdered milk

$1/3$ cup shortening

Stir dry ingredients together in a large bowl. Cut in shortening until mixture resembles fine meal. Store in a tightly sealed container. This mix will keep for a year.

I mix up 2–3 gallon-size containers at a time and use for biscuits, hot cakes, dumplings, and cake mixes by adding seasonings and flavorings. The amount of liquid you add will be important. Thin for hot cakes, a little thicker for waffles, and sticky dough for biscuits and muffins. You can add blueberries and other fruit for muffins. Baking pans and baking times will vary. Follow directions from biscuit recipes or muffin recipes for times to bake. This mix is great for a camping trip.

TIP: Using your Dutch oven in your kitchen oven with the lid on will produce a moist biscuit. You can even lower the heat to 300 degrees. Place your Dutch oven on a baking sheet if it has legs to keep it from falling through the shelf.

Dry Baking Mix Biscuits

2 cups Dry Baking Mix (see page 12)

$^1/_2$ cup water

Melted butter, optional

Preheat kitchen oven to 325 degrees or prepare 23–26 coals for cooking outside using a Dutch oven. Lightly grease a 12-inch Dutch oven.

In a medium bowl, combine baking mix and water until all liquid has been absorbed. Pat out dough or roll on a floured surface, leaving dough about $^1/_2$-inch thick. Cut using biscuit cutter or soup can. Place biscuits in Dutch oven. Brush tops of biscuits with melted butter, if desired.

Bake for 10–15 minutes in either your kitchen oven or use 7–8 coals on the bottom and 16–18 on the top of your Dutch oven. Wait for the smell to know the biscuits are done. Makes about 12 biscuits.

Granny's Country Biscuits

1 cup flour

3 heaping teaspoons baking powder

1 teaspoon salt

2 tablespoons shortening

1 cup milk or buttermilk

Preheat kitchen oven to 300 degrees. Grease a baking sheet.

In a medium bowl, mix together the dry ingredients and then cut in the shortening until it resembles coarse crumbs. Add the milk and mix well. If necessary, add enough flour to make a firm dough. Turn out of bowl onto a floured cutting board and pat out to about 1/2-inch thick. Cut in any shape, place on prepared baking sheet, and bake for about 15–20 minutes. When you can smell the bread, you know it's done. Makes 10–12 biscuits.

Raise 'em High Biscuits

3 cups flour

4 teaspoons baking powder

2 tablespoons sugar

$^1/_2$ teaspoon salt

$^3/_4$ teaspoon cream of tartar

$^1/_2$ cup butter

1 egg, beaten

1 cup milk

Preheat kitchen oven to 325 degrees or prepare 24 coals for cooking outside using a Dutch oven. Warm and grease a 12-inch cast iron skillet or a 12-inch Dutch oven.

In a large bowl, combine the dry ingredients and mix with a fork. Cut in the butter until the mixture looks like coarse cornmeal. Mix egg and milk together and add to dry mix. Beat only enough to moisten the dry ingredients. Place dough on a floured cutting board and knead lightly. Roll out to about 1-inch thick and cut into pieces using a biscuit cutter. Place in prepared skillet or Dutch oven. Bake for 15–20 minutes in your kitchen oven or use 8 coals on the bottom and 16 coals on the top of your Dutch oven. Makes approximately 20 biscuits.

Sour Milk Biscuits

2 cups flour

1 teaspoon salt

$^1/_4$ teaspoon baking soda

2 teaspoons baking powder

$^1/_4$ cup shortening

1 cup sour milk or buttermilk

Preheat kitchen oven to 350 degrees or prepare 22–23 coals for cooking outside using a Dutch oven. Grease a baking sheet or warm and grease a 12-inch Dutch oven.

In a large bowl, mix or sift together all dry ingredients. Cut in the shortening. Add the milk and work lightly to moisten all the flour. Drop dough by tablespoon on prepared baking sheet and bake for about 15–20 minutes until golden brown.

If using a Dutch oven, place biscuits in prepared Dutch oven and bake 20–25 minutes in your kitchen oven or use 7 coals on the bottom and 15–16 coals on the top of your Dutch oven. The smell will tell you when they are done. These biscuits will be moist and have a great taste. Makes 12–16 biscuits.

Cream Soda Biscuits

4 cups self-rising flour

$^1/_3$ cup vegetable oil

1 (12-ounce) can cream soda

$^1/_2$ teaspoon baking soda

$^1/_2$ teaspoon salt

Preheat kitchen oven to 350 degrees or prepare 24–26 coals for cooking outside using a Dutch oven. Grease a baking sheet or warm and grease a 12-inch Dutch oven.

Mix all ingredients together in a large bowl to make a soft dough. Roll out on a lightly floured board to about $^1/_2$-inch thick. Cut with a biscuit cutter or an open, clean soup can. Place the biscuits onto prepared baking sheet or in Dutch oven and bake about 20–25 minutes in either your kitchen oven or use 9–10 coals on the bottom and 15–16 coals on the top of your Dutch oven. The biscuits should be golden brown on the top when done. Makes 24–30 biscuits.

Cheesy Cheese Biscuits

1 cup flour

1 $^1/_2$ teaspoons baking powder

$^1/_2$ teaspoon salt

2 $^1/_2$ teaspoons shortening

$^3/_4$ cup grated cheese, of choice

$^1/_4$ cup chopped pimiento or chopped green onions

$^1/_3$ cup buttermilk or sour milk

Preheat kitchen oven to 300 degrees or prepare 24–25 coals for cooking outside using a Dutch oven. Warm and grease a 12-inch Dutch oven.

Sift first 3 ingredients into a large bowl. Cut in shortening until crumbly. Stir in remaining ingredients. Roll out on floured surface and cut with a biscuit cutter. Place biscuits in prepared Dutch oven and bake for 20 minutes in either your kitchen oven or use 9 coals on the bottom and 15–16 coals on the top of your Dutch oven. The bread smell will tell you when it's done. Makes 8–12 biscuits.

Variation: Lightly sprinkle the top of the biscuits with 1 teaspoon seasoned salt or garlic pepper before baking for a really great taste.

Bacon, Cheese, and Onion Biscuits

2 (10-count) cans refrigerated biscuits *

2 teaspoons vegetable oil or melted butter

$^1/_2$ teaspoon Log Cabin Grub All-Purpose Seasoning or all-purpose seasoning

1 pound bacon, cooked and crumbled

1 cup grated cheddar-jack cheese mix

$^1/_2$ cup chopped green onions

Preheat kitchen oven to 300 degrees or prepare 24 coals for cooking outside using a Dutch oven. Grease a 9 x 13-inch pan or warm and grease a 12-inch Dutch oven.

Arrange the biscuits on the bottom of prepared pan or Dutch oven. Brush or spray the tops of the biscuits with the oil. Sprinkle the seasoning on top of the biscuits and cover with bacon, cheese, and onions. Bake for 15 minutes in either your kitchen oven or use 8 coals on the bottom and 16 coals on the top of your Dutch oven. You'll know it's done when you can smell the bread and bacon. Makes 20 servings.

*You can also use your own baking powder biscuit mix from scratch or use any one of the recipes found in this book.

Fast-and-Fluffy
Sweet Potato Biscuits

1 (16-ounce) can sweet potatoes

3 cups flour

¹/₄ cup packed brown sugar

1 tablespoon baking powder

¹/₂ teaspoon each cinnamon and nutmeg, optional

1 ¹/₂ teaspoons salt

¹/₂ teaspoon baking soda

¹/₃ cup butter-flavor shortening

1 ³/₄ cups buttermilk

Preheat kitchen oven to 400 degrees or prepare 26–27 coals for cooking outside using a Dutch oven. Warm and grease a 12-inch Dutch oven.

Drain sweet potatoes, cut into half-inch chunks, and set aside. In a medium bowl, combine flour, brown sugar, baking powder, spices, salt, and baking soda. With a pastry blender, cut in shortening until mixture resembles coarse crumbs. Stir sweet potatoes and buttermilk into flour mixture just until ingredients are blended. Drop biscuits by heaping tablespoons, about 1 inch apart, in the bottom of the prepared Dutch oven. Bake for about 20 minutes in either your kitchen oven or use 9 coals on the bottom and 17–18 coals on the top of your Dutch oven. The smell will tell you when it's done and the biscuits will be golden brown. Makes 24–30 biscuits.

Sweet Twist Potato Biscuits

³/₄ cup mashed sweet potatoes

²/₃ cup milk

4 tablespoons butter, melted

1 ¹/₄ cups flour

1 teaspoon apple pie spice

4 teaspoons baking powder

1 tablespoon sugar

¹/₂ teaspoon salt

Preheat kitchen oven to 400 degrees. Grease a muffin tin.

In a large bowl, combine the sweet potatoes with milk and butter; mix well. Add dry ingredients in order given, mixing in after each addition, to form soft dough. Drop dough into muffin cups and bake for about 20 minutes or until you can smell them. These biscuits make a great side dish. Makes 12 biscuits.

Variation: Dough can be turned out onto floured board, tossed until smooth on outside, then rolled out ¹/₂-inch thick and cut with biscuit cutter. Place biscuits on greased baking sheet and bake for about 20 minutes.

Parker House Rolls

1 cup milk

5 tablespoons sugar

1/4 teaspoon nutmeg

1 tablespoon salt

1 package dry yeast

1 cup lukewarm water

6 cups sifted flour, divided

6 tablespoons shortening, melted

3 tablespoons butter, melted

Preheat kitchen oven to 325 degrees. Warm and grease a 12-inch Dutch oven.

In a small saucepan, scald milk and then add sugar, nutmeg, and salt; cool to lukewarm. Dissolve yeast in water and add to milk. Transfer mixture to a large bowl and add 3 cups flour and beat until perfectly smooth. Add shortening and enough flour to make easily handled dough. Knead well for 2–3 minutes until the dough is smooth and shiny; place in a large greased bowl. Cover and let rise until double in size, about 20–30 minutes.

Roll out dough to about 3/8-inch thick with a floured rolling pin and cut with a greased round glass or wide mouth bottle. Crease heavily through the center with a dull-edge knife and brush very lightly with butter. Fold in pocketbook shape and place close together in prepared Dutch oven. Cover and let rise for about 30 minutes. Place in kitchen oven and bake for about 25 minutes. The smell will tell you when they are done. Makes 36–40 rolls.

TIP: Remember, every minute you spend angry, mad, or upset is 60 seconds of happiness you'll never get back.

Mom's Potato-Water Rolls

2 packages dry yeast

1 cup leftover potato water from cooking potatoes

5 tablespoons sugar, divided

2 teaspoons salt

6 tablespoons butter, melted

6 cups enriched flour

3 tablespoons vegetable oil

Preheat kitchen oven to 300 degrees. Warm and grease a 12-inch Dutch oven.

In a large bowl, dissolve the yeast in lightly warmed potato water with 1 tablespoon sugar and let stand for 15 minutes. Add remaining sugar, salt, and butter and lightly blend together. Add flour and mix until a fairly stiff dough forms. Use more flour, if needed. Turn dough out onto a floured board and knead well. Knead for 2–3 minutes or until dough appears smooth and elastic looking. Spanking your bread helps to remove air pockets. Place in a large greased bowl and let double in size, about 30–45 minutes.

Punch down dough and make into 1-inch balls. Place the rolls inside the prepared Dutch oven. Grease the underneath side of the lid and place on the Dutch oven. Check after 20 minutes, the rolls will double in size again. Place the Dutch oven in your kitchen oven and bake for about 35 minutes. The smell will tell you when it is done. Brush rolls with oil and let stand for 10 minutes before serving. Makes 36–40 rolls.

Variation: You can also make 2 loaves of bread using this recipe. Preheat your kitchen oven to 300 degrees and grease 2 loaf pans. Divide the dough in half and place in prepared pans. Let sit, covered, until double in size. Bake for 30–35 minutes. The strong smell of the yeast will tell you when it's done.

Idaho Potato Rolls

1 package active dry yeast

1 cup warm water

2 eggs

$1/3$ cup sugar

1 teaspoon salt

$1/3$ cup vegetable oil

$1\,1/2$ cups warm mashed potatoes

$1/2$ cup nonfat dry milk

5 cups flour

3 tablespoons melted butter or oil

Preheat your kitchen oven to 400 degrees and grease a 12-inch Dutch oven.

Sprinkle yeast into warm water and let stand for 10 minutes. Combine eggs, sugar, salt, oil, potatoes, milk, and yeast mixture in a large bowl and mix well. Add 2 cups flour and beat well. Mix in remaining flour. Let rise for 30–40 minutes or until double in size.

Punch down and roll dough on a floured surface to about 1-inch thick. Cut with a floured biscuit cutter. Place rolls in prepared Dutch oven and brush top with butter or oil. Bake for about 25 minutes. Makes about 36 rolls.

Potato Bread

2 medium potatoes, peeled	**2 packages dry yeast**
1 1/2 cups water	**1/4 cup lukewarm water**
1/2 cup shortening, melted	**2 eggs, beaten and combined with enough milk to make 1 cup**
3/4 cup sugar	**6 cups sifted flour**
2 teaspoon salt	

Preheat kitchen oven to 325 degrees. Grease 2 loaf pans or warm and grease a 12-inch Dutch oven.

Boil potatoes until tender and drain, reserving 1 1/2 cups cooking water. In a large bowl, mash potatoes with 1/2 cup potato water. Add shortening to remaining warm potato water and mix well with the mashed potatoes. Add sugar and salt and mix well again.

Dissolve yeast in lukewarm water. Once dissolved, add yeast mixture to potato mixture and blend well. Allow to cool and then add egg mixture. Add flour a little at a time to make a soft dough. Place dough on a lightly floured board and knead for 10 minutes. Spanking or slapping the dough will remove the air pockets. Place dough in a large greased bowl, cover, and allow to rise until double in size, about 30 minutes. Punch down and place on a floured board and knead lightly a few more times. Divide dough into 2 equal loaves and place into prepared loaf pans, or, if using a Dutch oven, place 2 loaves in the Dutch oven side by side. Allow another 30 minutes for the dough to double in size again. Bake for 25–30 minutes. Cool on a wire rack. Makes 2 loaves.

Variations: You can make 1 large loaf by not dividing the dough into 2 loaves and following the above instructions. Bake for 45–50 minutes. You can also shape the dough into 20–25 dinner rolls and arrange them in your Dutch oven. Bake for 30–35 minutes.

Quick Potato Bread

4 1/2 cups warm water

2 packages dry yeast

4 tablespoons sugar

6 tablespoons vegetable oil

1 tablespoon salt

1 1/2 cups instant potato flakes

8 to 10 cups flour, divided

Preheat kitchen oven to 325 degrees. Warm and lightly grease 2 (12-inch) Dutch ovens.

Pour water in a large bowl and sprinkle yeast over the top. Allow to dissolve completely. Add sugar, oil, salt, instant potatoes, and 5 cups flour. Combine until smooth. Add remaining flour to make moderately stiff dough. Knead until smooth and satiny. Place dough in a large greased bowl and turn to coat. Cover and allow to rise until double in size, about 30 minutes. Punch down and divide into 4 loaves. Place 2 loaves in each Dutch oven and bake for 35 minutes. Makes 4 loaves.

Streamlined White Bread

1 package dry yeast

1 $1/4$ cups warm water

2 tablespoons shortening, softened

2 teaspoons salt

2 tablespoons sugar

3 cups flour, divided

Preheat kitchen oven to 325 degrees. Grease 2 loaf pans or warm and grease a 12-inch Dutch oven.

In a large bowl, dissolve yeast in warm water. Add shortening, salt, sugar, and half the flour. Beat for about 2 minutes. Add remaining flour. Place dough in a large greased bowl, cover, and let rise in a warm place for 30–45 minutes. Stir down batter. Divide into prepared pans. Batter will be sticky. Let rise for about 45 minutes. If using a Dutch oven, pour in the batter, grease the underside of the lid, and cover. Let rise for 20–25 minutes. Bake for 40–45 minutes. The bread smell will let you know it's done. Makes 15–20 servings.

Easy, Easy Beer Bread

5 cups self-rising flour, divided

1 tablespoon baking powder

1 teaspoon salt

3 tablespoons sugar

1 $^1/_2$ cups beer, room temperature

3 tablespoons vegetable oil

Preheat kitchen oven to 325 degrees or prepare 23–24 coals for cooking outside using a Dutch oven. Grease 2 loaf pans or warm and grease a 12-inch Dutch oven for a large round sheep-herder style loaf.

Mix 3 cups flour, baking powder, salt, and sugar in a large bowl. Add beer and oil; mix well. On a lightly floured surface, work in the remaining flour until a sticky dough is formed. Return to the bowl and let rise until double in size. Punch down and place in prepared pans or Dutch oven. Allow to rise until double in size, about 25–30 minutes.

Bake for 35 minutes in either your kitchen oven or use 8 coals on the bottom and 15–16 coals on the top of your Dutch oven. Unless the wind is blowing, you will not need to replace the coals. Makes 24–30 servings.

Cornbread
with Pork Rind

1 1/2 cups cornmeal

1/2 cup flour

1/2 cup crumbled pork rinds

2 tablespoons baking powder

1/2 teaspoon salt

1 egg, beaten

1 1/2 cups buttermilk

Preheat kitchen oven to 300 degrees. Warm and grease a 9 x 13-inch pan, a 12-inch Dutch oven, or a 12-inch cast iron skillet.

Place all dry ingredients in a large bowl and fluff together with a fork. Mix the egg with the buttermilk and add to dry ingredients; beat well with a fork and pour into prepared pan of choice. You can cover your Dutch oven for a very moist bread or leave uncovered, if you desire. Place in oven and bake for about 35 minutes. When you smell it, it is usually done. Makes 12–16 servings.

TIP: You can stick a tooth pick in the center of the bread and if it comes out clean, it is ready. Or you can lightly touch the middle of the bread with your finger to see if it springs back. If it doesn't spring back, it isn't done yet.

Mama's Best Cornbread

1 cup flour

2 cups cornmeal

1 teaspoon salt

4 teaspoons baking powder

1 tablespoon sugar

$^1/_2$ teaspoon cream of tartar

1 egg

1 cup milk or buttermilk

Preheat your kitchen oven to 300 degrees and grease a 12-inch cast iron skillet, a 12-inch Dutch oven, or corn stick pans.

Combine all the dry ingredients in a large bowl and mix together. Then add the egg and milk. You should have a moderately thin batter. Pour into your prepared pan and bake for approximately 30–35 minutes in your kitchen oven. The baking time might not take as long if you use corn stick pans. The smell will let you know it's done. Makes 20–24 servings.

TIP: Cornbread was always a real treat when Mama made it from scratch. So I'm honored to share a great old recipe from the farm. Your best flavor will come from using a cast iron pan, but you can use a 9 x 13-inch pan or muffin tins to make 24 muffins.

Mama Belle's Corn Fritters

2 cups corn oil

2 eggs

1 (15-ounce) can creamed corn

1 teaspoon baking powder

$^1/_2$ teaspoon salt

Dash of pepper

1 cup buttermilk

1 cup flour (can be $^1/_2$ cornmeal)

Heat oil in a deep skillet or an 8-inch Dutch oven to 400 degrees (use a thermometer).

Beat the eggs in a large bowl and add the corn. Mix in baking powder, salt, pepper, and buttermilk. Add the flour $^1/_2$ cup at a time and mix until well blended. Drop by teaspoonfuls into hot oil for deep frying. Brown on one side and turn over with a long handled fork. Remove from oil and drain on a rack or paper towel. Repeat the process until batter is used up. Makes approximately 20–24 fritters.

TIP: Using a basket ladle strainer is the best way to remove fritters from the oil.

Quick-and-Easy Chili and Cornbread

1 1/2 pounds lean ground beef

1 onion, chopped

3 cups cooked pinto or red beans

1 (32-ounce) jar of garlic and herb spaghetti sauce

1/2 teaspoon garlic powder

3 tablespoons chili powder

1 teaspoon thyme

1/2 teaspoon salt

1/4 teaspoon pepper

Mama's Best Cornbread (see page 30), unbaked

Preheat kitchen oven to 300 degrees or prepare 22 coals for cooking outside using a Dutch oven.

Sauté beef and onions in the bottom of a 12-inch Dutch oven until beef is cooked through. Add all remaining ingredients and simmer for 10–15 minutes while you mix up your cornbread. Spread the cornbread mixture over the top of the chili. Place the lid on Dutch oven and bake in your kitchen oven for 20 minutes. If cooking outside, use 7 coals on the bottom and 15 coals on the top of your Dutch oven. Wait for the smell and you will know when it is done. It should take about 20 minutes. Great served with tortilla chips and green salad. Makes 15–20 servings.

Apple-Carrot Harvest Bread

2 1/2 cups flour

1 cup sugar

1 teaspoon baking powder

1/2 teaspoon baking soda

1 teaspoon cinnamon

1/2 teaspoon salt

1/2 teaspoon nutmeg

1/4 teaspoon cloves

3 eggs

1/2 cup vegetable oil

1/2 cup milk

1 large apple, peeled and diced

1/2 cup shredded carrots

1/2 cup raisins, currants, or cranberries

Cinnamon, optional

Sugar, optional

Preheat kitchen oven to 325 degrees. Warm, grease, and flour a 12-inch Dutch oven.

Combine flour, sugar, baking powder, baking soda, cinnamon, salt, nutmeg, and cloves in a large bowl. Set aside. Combine eggs, oil, and milk in a small bowl. Add wet ingredients to dry ingredients and mix well. Fold in apple, carrots, and raisins. Pour batter in Dutch oven. You can sprinkle the top with cinnamon and sugar, if you like. Bake for about 50 minutes. You will know by the smell when it's done. Makes 12–16 servings.

Spiced Apple Nut Bread

1 cup flour

$1/2$ teaspoon salt

$1/2$ teaspoon cinnamon

2 teaspoons baking powder

$1/2$ teaspoon baking soda

$1/4$ teaspoon nutmeg

1 cup grated apple

$1/2$ cup applesauce

$1/3$ cup butter, softened

$2/3$ cup packed brown sugar

2 eggs

1 cup whole wheat flour

1 cup chopped nuts, of choice, divided

Preheat kitchen oven to 325 degrees. Warm and grease a 12-inch Dutch oven or a 9 x 13-inch baking pan.

Combine flour, salt, cinnamon, baking powder, baking soda, and nutmeg in a medium bowl and set aside. Combine apple and applesauce and set aside.

In a large bowl, cream together butter, brown sugar, and eggs. Stir half of the flour mixture into the butter mixture. Add apple mixture and add the rest of the flour mixture. Add the whole wheat flour to the heavy batter mixture and stir in $1/2$ cup nuts. Pour batter into the prepared Dutch oven and top with remaining $1/2$ cup nuts. Bake for about 1 hour. Let stand 10 minutes and then cool on a wire rack. Makes 12–16 servings.

Variation: This bread is very good served warm with caramel topping and whipped cream.

Spicy Applesauce Nut Bread

2 cups flour

$3/4$ cup sugar

3 tablespoons baking powder

$1/2$ teaspoon baking soda

$1/2$ teaspoon salt

$1/2$ teaspoon cinnamon

$1/4$ teaspoon nutmeg

$1/4$ teaspoon cloves

1 egg, beaten

1 cup applesauce

$1/4$ cup sour milk or buttermilk

2 tablespoons shortening, melted

1 cup chopped walnuts or pecans

Preheat kitchen oven to 300 degrees or prepare 21–22 coals for cooking outside using a Dutch oven. Warm and grease a 10-inch Dutch oven.

Sift flour, sugar, baking powder, baking soda, salt, and spices into a large bowl. Set aside. Combine remaining ingredients in a medium bowl and pour into flour mixture. Stir just enough to moisten. Place batter in prepared Dutch oven and bake for 1 hour or until done in your kitchen oven or use 8 coals on the bottom and 13–14 coals on the top of your Dutch oven. You will know by the smell when it's done. Be sure your coals are in a circle under the outside edge of your Dutch oven. Baking low and slow will keep the moisture in the bread. Makes 10 servings.

Variation: Add $1/2$ cup raisins, cranberries, or candied fruits along with the nuts.

Grated Zucchini Bread

1 cup sugar

1 cup packed brown sugar

3 eggs

1 cup vegetable oil

2 cups grated zucchini

1 tablespoon vanilla

3 cups flour

1 teaspoon salt

1 teaspoon baking soda

1 tablespoon cinnamon

$^1/_4$ teaspoon baking powder

$^1/_2$ teaspoon nutmeg

$^1/_2$ cups chopped nuts, of choice

Preheat your kitchen oven to 325 degrees. Grease 2 small loaf pans or warm and grease a 10-inch Dutch oven.

In a large bowl, combine sugars, eggs, oil, zucchini, and vanilla. Sift the dry ingredients together in a medium bowl; stir in nuts. Add to the zucchini mixture just until the flour is mixed in. Pour into prepared pans and bake for 50–60 minutes. The smell will make your eyes water. Makes 12–16 servings.

Breakfasts

Biscuit and Ham Bake

2 tablespoons butter

10 eggs, beaten

1 (5-ounce) can evaporated milk

1 teaspoon prepared mustard

8 ounces cheddar cheese, cubed

3/4 cup cubed cooked ham

1 (10-count) can refrigerated flaky buttermilk biscuits

Preheat kitchen oven to 325 degrees.

Melt butter in a deep 12-inch cast iron skillet; add eggs, milk, mustard, and cheese and stir constantly, over low heat, until the eggs are set. Add ham and gently stir. Separate the biscuits and pull apart in half. Place halved biscuits around the top of the skillet on the egg mixture. Bake, uncovered, in your oven for 15–20 minutes or until biscuits are golden brown. Makes 10–12 servings.

Variation: Use cooked bacon bits or sausage to replace ham or you can use a combination of all three meats.

TIP: To make bacon bits, cut the bacon in small pieces before frying. It will fry more evenly that way.

Biscuit Breakfast

1 1/2 cups flour

1 tablespoon baking powder

1 tablespoon sugar

1 teaspoon salt

1/4 cup shortening

3/4 cup milk or light cream

6 eggs, beaten

1 tablespoon butter

6 slices American cheese

6 slices cooked ham

Preheat kitchen oven to 375 degrees and warm and lightly grease a 12-inch Dutch oven.

In a large bowl, combine dry ingredients; cut in shortening until crumbly—or you can just use 2 cups of Bisquick. Stir in milk just until moistened. Turn onto a lightly floured surface; knead 5– 6 times. Roll to 1-inch thickness and cut 6 biscuits with a biscuit cutter.

Place biscuits in prepared Dutch oven and bake for 12–15 minutes or until light golden brown; cool slightly. You'll know they are done by the smell. While biscuits are cooling, scramble eggs in a medium skillet over medium heat in butter until completely set. Split the biscuits; place cheese, hot eggs, and ham on bottoms. Replace tops and serve. Makes 6 servings.

Blueberry Sour Cream Pancakes

2 cups flour

1/4 cup sugar

4 teaspoons baking powder

1/2 teaspoon salt

2 eggs

1 1/2 cups milk

1 cup sour cream

2 tablespoons butter, softened

1 cup blueberries, fresh or frozen

Combine dry ingredients in a large bowl. In a medium bowl, beat eggs. Add milk, sour cream, and butter; mix well. Stir into dry ingredients just until blended. Fold in blueberries. Using 1/4 cup, pour batter onto a greased hot griddle; turn when bubbles form on top of pancakes. Cook until the second side is golden brown. Serve with blueberry sauce. Makes approximately 20 pancakes.

Blueberry Sauce

1/2 cup sugar

2 tablespoons cornstarch

1/2 cup water

4 cups fresh or frozen blueberries

In a medium saucepan, combine sugar and cornstarch. Gradually stir in water. Add blueberries; bring to a boil over medium heat and boil for 2 minutes, stirring constantly. Remove from heat, cover, and keep warm. Makes 3 1/2 cups.

Hootenanny Pancakes

6 eggs

1 cup milk

$1/4$ teaspoon cream of tartar

$1/2$ teaspoon baking powder

$1/2$ teaspoon salt

1 cup flour

1 cup butter

In a large bowl, combine eggs, milk, cream of tartar, baking powder, and salt; beat until fluffy. Add flour, a little at a time, beating until well blended. Melt butter in a small saucepan. When butter is melted, pour into batter all at once and thoroughly mix. Using $1/4$ cup, pour batter onto a greased hot griddle; turn when bubbles form on top of pancakes. Cook until the second side is golden brown. Serve immediately. Top with syrup, honey, or jam. Also tastes great with lemon juice and powdered sugar. Makes approximately 20 pancakes.

Variation: Additions of fruit or chocolate chips are great or you can sour the milk with a splash of vinegar for that sour dough taste. Be sure to warm your griddle before placing batter on it or pancakes will stick.

TIP: If your griddle constantly sticks, put a cup of white vinegar on it and let it simmer dry. Warm the griddle and then grease it before using.

Quick Sourdough Pancakes

1 egg

1 teaspoon salt

1 tablespoon sugar

1 $1/2$ cups sourdough starter mix

$1/4$ teaspoon nutmeg

$1/4$ teaspoon cinnamon

$1/2$ cup flour

1 teaspoon cream of tartar

$1/2$ teaspoon baking soda

2 tablespoons warm water

Heat a griddle on your kitchen stove to about 400 degrees.

In a large bowl, mix all ingredients together except the baking soda and water. Combine the baking soda and water together in a small cup and stir into the batter just enough to combine ingredients. Allow the batter to double in size. This should take about 10 minutes. Ladle batter onto hot griddle using about $1/4$ cup per pancake. Turn when bubbles pop and do not refill the hole. Batter may thicken as it sits, so just add a little water to make the batter pour easily. Pancakes are done when golden brown. Makes approximately 20 pancakes.

Variations: Add some berries or fruit to the batter just before cooking. Adding bacon bits is tasty. This recipe will also work great in old-fashioned waffle irons or old electric ones. Be sure the iron is hot and lightly oiled before you pour in the batter.

Dutch Oven French Toast

2 cups light cream or milk

4 eggs

2 tablespoons sugar

1 teaspoon vanilla

1 teaspoon cinnamon

$1/8$ teaspoon nutmeg

6 cups bread cubes, dry or fresh

Preheat kitchen oven to 325 degrees. Warm and grease a 12-inch Dutch oven.

In a large bowl, combine all the ingredients except the bread cubes; mix well. Stir in the bread cubes and allow to sit for 10 minutes, or until all the liquid has been absorbed. Spoon into prepared Dutch oven and bake for 45–50 minutes or until you can smell the spices. Remove from the Dutch oven and slice. Serve with hot syrup of your choice and a sprinkling of powdered sugar for appearance, if desired. Makes 6–8 servings.

Variation: You can add apple, blueberry, or any fruit pie filling to the egg mix before adding bread cubes.

New Orleans Fried French Toast

1 1/4 cups oil

10 slices day-old bread

1/2 cup butter, softened

3/4 cup packed brown sugar

1 3/4 cups flour

1/2 teaspoon nutmeg

1/2 teaspoon cinnamon

1 1/2 teaspoons baking powder

1/2 teaspoon salt

2 eggs

1 cup milk

3 tablespoons melted butter

Powdered sugar

Heat oil in 10-inch cast iron skillet to about 400–425 degrees.

Spread bread with softened butter. Sprinkle 5 slices with brown sugar, using about 2 tablespoons on each. Cover these slices with the other buttered slices, making sandwiches. Cut each into quarters.

In a medium bowl, sift together flour, spices, baking powder, and salt. Add eggs, milk, and melted butter. Mix well. Dip each sandwich quarter into batter. Cook sandwiches in hot oil on both sides until brown, turning only once. Sprinkle with powdered sugar; serve with tart jelly and a platter of crisp bacon. Makes 10 servings.

Stuffed Blueberry French Toast

6 eggs

1 teaspoon grated orange peel

$2/3$ cup milk

3 tablespoons sugar

$1/4$ teaspoon salt

8 slices thick Texas Toast bread

1 cup fresh or frozen blueberries, thawed and drained

$1/2$ cup sliced almonds, optional

Preheat and grease a griddle.

In a medium bowl, beat eggs, orange peel, milk, sugar, and salt until well blended. With the tip of a sharp knife, cut a 1 1/2-inch wide pocket in the side of each bread slice. Fill pockets with blueberries, dividing evenly. Place filled slices in egg mixture, coating evenly on both sides. Arrange bread on prepared griddle. Sprinkle with almonds. Cook until golden brown, turning to brown on both sides. Makes 8 servings.

Variation: Any pie filling can be substituted for the blueberries.

Dutch Oven Bacon and Eggs

- **2 pounds bacon**
- **1 large chopped onion**
- **2 pounds hash browns**
- **1 red bell pepper, chopped, optional**
- **1 green bell pepper, chopped, optional**
- **12 eggs**
- **1 tablespoon Log Cabin Grub All-Purpose Seasoning or all-purpose seasoning, of choice**
- **2 cups grated cheddar cheese**

Preheat kitchen oven to 325 degrees or prepare 25 coals for cooking outside using a Dutch oven.

Cut bacon into small pieces and brown until crisp in the bottom of a 12-inch Dutch oven. Pour off part of the grease and add the onion. Sauté and add hash browns and bell peppers, if using. Stir and allow to cook for a few minutes. Pour cracked eggs on top, or beat eggs, and mix in. Sprinkle top with seasoning and cheese. Cover and bake for about 20 minutes in your kitchen oven or until eggs are done, or use 10 coals on the bottom and 15 coals on the top of your Dutch oven. If you wait for the smell, it will take the same amount of time. This is great served with salsa or warm chili. Makes 12–15 servings.

Chuck Wagon Scrambled Eggs

1 cup canned tomatoes, with liquid

1 cup canned corn, drained

6 eggs

Salt and pepper, to taste

Heat and lightly grease a 12-inch cast iron skillet.

Stir in tomatoes and corn (fresh tomatoes and corn can be used in season). Heat mixture and add eggs. Stir enough to break the yolks and season with salt and pepper. Stir and cook until eggs are scrambled, about 8–10 minutes. Make 6 servings.

Variations: Add mushrooms, bacon bits, ham pieces, sausage, hamburger, salsa, or cheese. Serve with cornbread or biscuits. Use your imagination and serve anything that sounds good to you.

Simple Mountain Man Breakfast

2 pounds ground sausage

1 medium onion or 3 green onions, chopped

5 to 6 large potatoes, boiled and diced

8 eggs

$1/2$ cup water or milk

1 cup grated cheddar cheese

Prepare 25 coals for cooking outside using a 12-inch Dutch oven.

Brown sausage and onions in Dutch oven; stir potatoes into the sausage mix and brown.

In a large bowl, beat the eggs and water thoroughly. Pour evenly over the potato mix. Sprinkle cheese on top. Cook for 15–20 minutes until eggs are firm using 10 coals on the bottom and 15 coals on the top of your Dutch oven. The smell will tell you when it is done. Makes 4–6 servings.

Cooking variation: You can also bake this recipe in your kitchen oven at 325 degrees for 15–20 minutes.

Country Bacon Skillet

12 bacon strips

6 cups cooked cubed potatoes

³/₄ cup chopped green bell pepper

¹/₂ cup chopped onion

¹/₂ cup shredded cabbage

1 teaspoon salt

¹/₄ teaspoon pepper

6 eggs

¹/₂ cup grated cheddar-jack cheese

¹/₂ cup chopped green onion

Over medium heat in a large 12-inch cast iron skillet, cook bacon until crisp. Remove bacon; crumble and set aside. Add potatoes, bell pepper, onion, cabbage, salt, and pepper to drippings. Cook and stir for 2 minutes. Cover and cook, stirring occasionally until potatoes are browned and tender, about 10 minutes. A piece of aluminum foil on top will be sufficient for a cover.

Make 6 wells in the potato mixture and break 1 egg into each well. Cover and cook for 8–10 minutes or until eggs are set. Sprinkle with cheese and bacon. A handful of chopped green onion makes it look real pretty. Makes 6 servings.

Skillet Breakfast Casserole

1 tablespoon vegetable oil

4 cups frozen tater tots, thawed

$^1/_2$ cup cooked and crumbled sausage

1 (3-ounce) package country gravy mix

1 $^1/_2$ cups water

2 large eggs

1 $^1/_2$ cups grated cheddar cheese

1 tablespoon chopped green onions

Preheat kitchen oven to 325 degrees. Preheat a 12-inch cast iron skillet on stove top and lightly grease.

Add tater tots and cook for 3–4 minutes until brown. Add sausage. In a large bowl, whisk gravy mix into water. Beat eggs into gravy mix. Pour evenly over tots in skillet. Bake for 25–30 minutes or until filling is set. Sprinkle cheese on top and allow to cook for another 3 minutes or until cheese is melted. Garnish with green onions. Makes 4–6 servings.

Cooking variation: You can also cook this recipe outside in a 12-inch Dutch oven using 10 coals on the bottom and 15 coals on the top of your Dutch oven for 25–30 minutes or until filling is set.

Hamburger Skillet Breakfast

1 pound ground beef

1 cup chopped uncooked bacon

1 (2-pound) package hash browns

6 to 8 eggs

Salt and pepper or Log Cabin Grub All-Purpose Seasoning, to taste

1 cup grated cheddar-jack cheese, optional

Warm and lightly grease a 12-inch cast iron skillet.

Crumble beef and bacon in the bottom and fry until cooked through. Add the hash browns. Stir the mixture until well combined and heated through. Break eggs over the top and cover. Steam or simmer for 5–10 minutes until the eggs are cooked as you like. Season, to taste. Cheese can also be sprinkled over the top. Serve with biscuits or rolls. Makes 6–8 servings.

Note: If you are feeding more, you can use up to 12 eggs on the top.

Cooking Variations: This recipe can be prepared in a 12-inch Dutch oven using the bottom as a deep frying pan. Cook this on your kitchen stove, outside on a camp stove, or over 18–20 coals. Remove 7–8 of the coals after cooking the meat and adding potatoes.

Breakfast Patties and Taters

$^1/_4$ cup water

2 teaspoons salt

2 teaspoons rubbed sage

1 teaspoon pepper

$^1/_2$ teaspoon nutmeg

$^1/_8$ teaspoon ground ginger

$^1/_2$ cup chopped red bell pepper

$^1/_2$ cup chopped green bell pepper

2 pounds ground pork

2 pounds thawed hash browns

Preheat kitchen oven to 300 degrees or prepare 23 coals for cooking outside using a Dutch oven. Warm and grease the bottom of a 12-inch Dutch oven.

In a large bowl, combine water and seasonings. Add the bell peppers and pork; mix well. Shape into patties. Place patties in prepared Dutch oven and cook for 5–6 minutes on each side or until no longer pink in the center. Place hash browns over the sausage and place the lid on Dutch oven. Bake for 20 minutes in your kitchen oven or use 8 coals on the bottom and 15 coals on the top of your Dutch oven until you can smell it. Makes 8–10 servings.

Breakfast Potato Boats

**8 leftover or freshly baked potatoes
or 8 cups leftover mashed or instant potatoes**

1 cup butter

2 cups grated cheddar cheese

1 cup chopped green onions

1 cup bacon bits

Salt and pepper, to taste

2 teaspoons paprika

1 teaspoon parsley

1 tablespoon Log Cabin Grub All-Purpose Seasoning

Preheat kitchen oven to 300 degrees or prepare 24 coals for cooking outside using a Dutch oven.

Make a slit in the potato and scoop out all the white potato meat, or make 8 potato-shaped boats out of aluminum foil for using mashed potatoes. In a large bowl, mix all ingredients except Log Cabin Grub Seasoning. Fill the boats with potato mix and sprinkle with seasoning.

Place the potato boats in a 9 x 13-inch pan or a 12-inch Dutch oven. Bake for 25–30 minutes in your kitchen oven or use 9 coals on the bottom and 15 coals on the top of your Dutch oven. You can sprinkle extra cheese on top with more bacon bits, if desired. Serve with hot rolls, biscuits, or pancakes. Makes 8 servings.

Variation: You can replace the bacon with sausage in this recipe for a different flavor.

Country Breakfast Pizza

1 (1-pound) package country pork sausage

1 (8-count) can refrigerated crescent rolls

1 cup frozen hash brown potato cubes, thawed

3 tablespoons diced red bell pepper

3 tablespoons diced yellow bell pepper

1/4 cup thinly sliced green onions, optional

1 cup grated cheddar or mozzarella cheese, divided

3 eggs, lightly beaten

3 tablespoons milk

1/2 teaspoon salt

1 teaspoon black pepper

Preheat oven to 325 degrees.

In 12-inch cast iron skillet, cook sausage over medium-high heat, stirring frequently until no longer pink. Remove from heat.

Separate rolls into 8 triangles. Place on an ungreased 12-inch rimmed pizza pan with points toward the center. Press together, seal perforations, and form a circle 1-inch larger in diameter than pan bottom. Turn edges under to make a slight rim. Sprinkle cooked sausage over crust. Top with potatoes. Add bell peppers and green onions. Sprinkle with 3/4 cup cheese.

Stir eggs, milk, salt, and pepper in small bowl; pour evenly over pizza. Sprinkle with remaining cheese. Bake 20 minutes or until eggs are set and crust is golden. Makes 8–10 servings.

Deviled Egg, Ham, and Asparagus Casserole

2 (15-ounce) cans asparagus

12 deviled eggs

2 cups cubed ham

2 (15-ounce) cans cheddar cheese soup or 1 can each cream of celery and cream of mushroom soup

$^1/_4$ cup milk

1 cup plain bread crumbs

Preheat kitchen oven to 325 degrees or prepare 25 coals for cooking outside using a Dutch oven. Warm and grease a 12-inch Dutch oven.

Let asparagus drain in a colander. Place asparagus in prepared Dutch oven. Top with ham. Place deviled eggs on top of ham, deviled side down. Mix soup and milk and pour over eggs. Top with bread crumbs and bake for 20 minutes in your kitchen oven or use 9 coals on the bottom and 16 coals on the top of your Dutch oven. Wait for the smell and it will tell you when it is done. Makes 8–10 servings.

TIP: Dutch ovens are actually like a pressure cooker. Under the heavy lid they form 1–3 pounds of pressure which release when the food is cooked and vents under the lid. If you can smell it, it's done.

Sweet Blueberry Spread

¹/₂ cup blueberries, fresh or frozen

¹/₂ cup honey, divided

¹/₄ cup butter, softened

Combine blueberries and 2 tablespoons honey in a small saucepan. Bring to boil, stirring constantly. Reduce heat and simmer, cook 3–4 minutes until mixture is thickened and reduced by half. Cool. Blend in remaining honey. Beat in butter. Great for toast and muffins. You can double the recipe and store in your refrigerator for 6–8 months. Great over hot cakes and waffles too. Makes 1 pint.

Side Dishes

Bean Salad Caviar

1 (15-ounce) can black-eyed peas, drained

1 (15-ounce) can pinto beans, drained

1 (15-ounce) can black beans, drained

1 (15-ounce) can garbanzo beans, drained

1 (4-ounce) can diced pimientos, drained

1 cup chopped celery

1 cup diced white or red onion

1 (4-ounce) can diced green chiles, drained

1 green bell pepper, diced

1 red bell pepper, diced

1 (5-ounce) jar diced jalapeno peppers, drained, optional

Combine all ingredients in large bowl and mix.

Dressing

1 teaspoon salt

$^1/_2$ teaspoon pepper

$^3/_4$ cup cider vinegar

$^1/_2$ cup vegetable oil

1 tablespoon water

1 cup sugar

Combine the dressing ingredients in a small saucepan and bring to a boil. Pour hot dressing over the bean mixture and refrigerate overnight. When ready to serve, drain liquid from the beans and serve with chips, on a bed of lettuce, or as a side dish. Makes 15–20 servings.

Calico Beans

1 pound bacon, cut in small pieces

1 pound ground beef

$^1/_2$ cup chopped sweet white onion

1 cup ketchup

1 tablespoon vinegar

1 cup molasses

1 teaspoon salt

1 cup packed brown sugar

$^1/_4$ cup prepared mustard

1 (15-ounce) can pork and beans, drained

1 (15-ounce) can garbanzo beans, drained

1 (15-ounce) can kidney beans, drained

1 (15-ounce) can hominy, drained

1 (15-ounce) can pinto beans, drained

Preheat kitchen oven to 325 degrees or prepare 22–24 coals for cooking outside using a Dutch oven.

Fry bacon in a 12-inch Dutch oven. Add beef and onion. When browned, add rest of ingredients and mix well. Cover and bake for 1 hour in your kitchen oven or use 10 coals on the bottom and 12–14 coals on the top of your Dutch oven. Makes approximately 20 servings.

Pineapple–
Dr. Pepper Beans

4 bell peppers, diced (green, yellow, and/or red)

2 medium red onions, diced

1 (15-ounce) can diced tomatoes with liquid

1 teaspoon Worcestershire sauce

1 pound summer sausage, sliced

4 (28-ounce) cans pork and beans, drained

2 (16-ounce) cans pineapple tidbits, drained

2 (12-ounce) cans Dr. Pepper

2 cups packed brown sugar

4 cloves garlic, chopped

Combine bell peppers, onions, and tomatoes and sauté in a 12-inch Dutch oven on your kitchen stove top or a camp stove until veggies are tender. Add remaining ingredients and stir to blend flavors and dissolve the brown sugar. Cook for 30 minutes. Makes 20–25 servings.

When I was a child, Dr. Pepper was called Ironport and Cherry. That's what my mama used. It is no longer available and Dr. Pepper or Cherry Coke work just fine.

Sweet Oriental Beans

4 (15-ounce) cans navy beans, drain 2 of them

1 cup chopped celery

2 large onions, diced

1 (4-ounce) jar chopped pimientos

1 red or yellow bell pepper, chopped

1 cup packed brown sugar

1 teaspoon celery salt

1 teaspoon salt

1 teaspoon soy sauce

1 tablespoon powdered mustard

Preheat kitchen oven to 300 degrees or prepare 19 coals for cooking outside using a Dutch oven.

Place beans, celery, and onions in 10-inch Dutch oven. Cover and simmer 10 minutes on your kitchen stove top or a camp stove. Combine pimientos and bell pepper and add to the beans. Add brown sugar, celery salt, salt, soy sauce, and mustard. Bake for 30 minutes in your kitchen oven or use 7 coals on the bottom and 12 coals on the top of your Dutch oven. You can also continue to simmer the beans on your camp stove. Makes 12–16 servings.

Uptown Green Beans

$^1/_2$ pound bacon, cut in small pieces

1 onion, diced

1 package Lit'l Smokies, chopped

1 tablespoon vegetable oil

4 cups fresh or frozen green beans

1 (10.75-ounce) can cream of mushroom soup

1 (4-ounce) jar pimientos, chopped, optional

2 cloves garlic, diced, or 2 teaspoons garlic powder

Parmesan cheese

Place bacon, onions, Lit'l Smokies, and garlic in oil in a 10-inch Dutch oven and sauté using your kitchen stove top. Add remaining ingredients and simmer for 30 minutes. Sprinkle with cheese before serving. Makes 8–10 servings.

Cooking variation: You can also bake this dish outside using 8 coals in a circle underneath the Dutch oven and 11 coals on the top.

Steamed Veggies

1 medium red onion, chopped

1 medium red bell pepper, chopped

1 medium green bell pepper, chopped

2 cups broccoli florets

2 cups chopped cauliflower

2 cups green beans

2 cups chopped yellow crookneck squash

2 cups chopped zucchini

2 cups chopped celery

1 cup water

$1/2$ teaspoon salt

Pepper, to taste

Preheat kitchen oven to 300 degrees or prepare 20 coals for cooking outside using a Dutch oven. Warm and lightly grease a 12-inch Dutch oven.

Place all vegetables in prepared Dutch oven and add water, salt, and pepper. Bake for about 20 minutes in your kitchen oven or use 8 coals on the bottom and 12 on the top of your Dutch oven. Do not cook longer than 20 minutes or the celery will go mushy. Makes 12–15 servings.

Variations: Sprinkle with all-purpose seasoning or garlic pepper for added taste. The vegetables are also very good served with a cheese sauce or white sauce.

Butter Creamed Cabbage

8 cups shredded cabbage

1 teaspoon salt

Water

1 cup heavy cream or evaporated milk

¹/₄ cup butter

Salt and pepper, to taste

¹/₂ cup diced green onion, optional

In a large saucepan, cook cabbage in salted water until just tender. Use enough water to cover the cabbage. Do not overcook. Drain the water and add cream and butter and continue to cook over low heat, stirring lightly until mixture is heated through. Do not boil. Season with salt and pepper, to taste. Sprinkle with green onions, if desired. Makes 6–10 servings.

Country Stuffed Mushrooms

1 pound Italian pork sausage

1 (8-ounce) package cream cheese

$1/2$ cup leftover cooked rice or bread crumbs

2 cloves garlic, crushed

20 medium mushrooms, stems removed

Prepare 25 coals for cooking outside using a Dutch oven or preheat your kitchen broiler. Warm and grease a 12-inch Dutch oven or a baking sheet with sides.

In a large cast iron skillet, brown sausage and mix in remaining ingredients, except for mushrooms. Use mixture to stuff in the mushrooms. Cook for 5–10 minutes with 10 coals on the bottom and 15 coals on the top of your Dutch oven. If using your kitchen broiler, place mushrooms on prepared baking sheet and broil for 3–5 minutes. Makes 20 mushrooms.

Variation: Use $1/2$ cup pork-flavored Stove Top Stuffing in place of rice or bread crumbs.

Cowboy Potatoes and Peas

5 strips bacon

2 large onions, sliced

8 medium potatoes, sliced or diced

1 teaspoon salt

$1/2$ teaspoon pepper

1 cup grated cheddar-jack cheese, divided

2 tablespoons Log Cabin Grub All-Purpose Seasoning or all-purpose seasoning

1 (16-ounce) package frozen peas

Prepare 25 coals for cooking outside using a Dutch oven in a volcano stove or preheat kitchen oven to 325 degrees. Warm and lightly grease a 12-inch Dutch oven.

Place the strips of bacon on the bottom of the prepared Dutch oven. Next place a layer of half of the onions and a layer of half of the potatoes. Salt and pepper the layer and sprinkle on $1/3$ of the cheese. Now lightly sprinkle with the seasoning. Repeat layers of onions, potatoes, cheese, and seasonings.

Place Dutch oven on your volcano on 12 coals and wait for the smell, about 45–50 minutes. At first smell, remove the lid and sprinkle on the remaining cheese and peas. Replace lid and let cook another 10 minutes. If it is a chilly day, you may need to replace the coals after 30 minutes.

If you are using your kitchen oven, place the covered Dutch oven in the kitchen oven and wait for the smell, about 35 minutes. Remove the lid and add remaining cheese and peas. Return to oven for 10 more minutes. Makes 10–12 servings.

TIP: Be sure to circle the coals under the outer rim of your Dutch oven.

Ginger-Glazed Carrots

10 carrots
¹/₄ cup butter
¹/₂ cup honey
2 tablespoons packed brown sugar
¹/₂ teaspoon ground ginger

Prepare 9 coals in a volcano stove for cooking outside using a Dutch oven.

Wash, peel, and slice carrots. Place a 12-inch Dutch oven in volcano and put butter in bottom to melt. Add carrots. Pour honey over the top and sprinkle with brown sugar. Lightly dust top with ginger. Cover and bake for 20 minutes. Remember to halfway close the damper of the volcano to preserve coals and keep the temperature around 350 degrees. Makes 8–10 servings.

TIP: Coals are ready to cook with when the edges start turning white, about 8–10 minutes.

Potato-Flakes Casserole

6 slices bacon, diced

1 medium onion, chopped

1 stick butter

1 (32-ounce) bag frozen hash brown cubes, thawed

2 (10.75-ounce) cans cream of chicken soup

2 cups sour cream

2$^1/_2$ cups cheddar-jack cheese

2 cups crumbled corn flakes

Preheat kitchen oven to 300 degrees or prepare 25 coals for cooking outside using a Dutch oven. Warm and grease a 12-inch Dutch oven.

In the prepared Dutch oven, cook bacon with the onions and butter until crisp, on your kitchen stove top or camp stove. Place potatoes in bacon grease and combine with bacon, onion, soup, sour cream, and cheese. Top with corn flakes and heat for 15–20 minutes to melt the cheese in your kitchen oven or use 10 coals on the bottom and 15 coals on the top of your Dutch oven. This is a great side dish for breakfast or lunch or dinner. Makes 10–12 servings.

Zucchini Casserole

6 (6-inch long) zucchini, sliced

2 tablespoons parsley flakes

1 teaspoon oregano

1 (16-ounce) can spaghetti or tomato sauce

$1/4$ cup butter

4 cups soft bread cubes

2 cups grated Parmesan cheese, divided

4 small tomatoes, sliced

$1/2$ pound mozzarella cheese, sliced

Preheat kitchen oven to 325 degrees and grease a 9 x 13-inch casserole dish.

In a large saucepan, boil zucchini until it is almost done, about 7–10 minutes; drain. Add parsley and oregano to the tomato sauce. Melt butter and toss bread cubes in a large skillet until cubes are brown.

Arrange food in the following order in prepared casserole dish: zucchini; $1/2$ of the sauce; evenly sprinkle $1/2$ of Parmesan cheese; $1/2$ of bread cubes; all of the mozzarella cheese; all of the tomatoes; remaining sauce; remaining Parmesan cheese; and remaining bread cubes on top.

Bake just long enough to warm through, about 20 minutes, or until casserole bubbles up. This is a fast side dish for any meal. Makes 12–15 servings.

Cheese and Cracker Zucchini Casserole

3 cups precooked thin egg noodles

1 (10.75-ounce) can vegetable soup

1 can water

2 teaspoons Worcestershire sauce

$1/2$ teaspoon salt

$1/2$ teaspoon oregano

1 pound zucchini, sliced

1 cup grated Swiss cheese, divided

$1/2$ cup smashed Ritz crackers, divided

Preheat kitchen oven to 325 degrees and grease a 10-inch Dutch oven.

Combine all ingredients except $1/2$ of the cheese and crackers. Cover and bake for 30 minutes. Stir then sprinkle remaining cheese and crackers on top. Bake 7–10 minutes longer. The smell will tell you it's done. Makes 8–10 servings.

Multi-Squash Casserole

2 cups (^{1}/4-inch thick) slices yellow summer squash

1 cup (^{1}/4-inch thick) slices zucchini

1 medium onion, chopped

^{1}/4 cup sliced green onions

1 cup water

1 teaspoon salt, divided

2 cups crushed butter-flavor crackers

^{1}/2 cup butter, melted

1 (10.75-ounce) can cream of chicken soup

1 large carrot, grated

^{1}/2 cup mayonnaise

1 (2-ounce) jar diced pimientos, drained

1 teaspoon ground sage

^{1}/2 teaspoon white pepper

1 cup grated cheddar-jack cheese

Preheat kitchen oven to 325 degrees or prepare 21 coals for cooking outside using a Dutch oven. Warm and lightly grease a 10-inch Dutch oven.

In a large saucepan, combine the first 5 ingredients; add ^{1}/2 teaspoon salt. Cover and cook until squash is tender, about 6 minutes. Drain well; set aside. Combine crackers and butter; spoon half into prepared Dutch oven. In a large bowl, combine soup, carrot, mayonnaise, pimientos, sage, pepper, and remaining salt; fold into squash mixture. Spoon over crumbs. Sprinkle with cheese and the remaining cracker mixture. Bake for 30 minutes or until lightly browned in your kitchen oven, or use 8 coals on the bottom and 13 coals on top of your Dutch oven. Makes 8–10 servings.

Aunt Joe's Tartar Sauce

1 cup mayonnaise

3 tablespoons finely diced onion

1 tablespoon sweet pickle relish

2 tablespoons dill pickle relish

1 teaspoon lemon juice

$1/_2$ teaspoon garlic salt

Salt and pepper, to taste

Place all ingredients in a small bowl and combine well. Refrigerate for at least 1 hour before using. Makes approximately 1 cup.

This sauce will keep for 3–4 months in the refrigerator.

Homemade Cocktail Sauce

1 cup ketchup

1 teaspoon horseradish

1 teaspoon lemon juice

Place all ingredients in a small bowl and combine well. Refrigerate for at least 1 hour before using. Makes 1 cup.

This sauce will keep for 6 months in the refrigerator.

Sweet-and-Sour Sauce

$1/3$ cup ketchup

$3/4$ cup sugar

1 tablespoon soy sauce

1 cup water, divided

$1/4$ cup vinegar

2 to 3 tablespoons cornstarch

Combine ketchup, sugar, soy sauce, and $2/3$ cup water in a small sauce pan and bring to a boil. Reduce the heat and stir often to keep from scorching. Add vinegar. Combine cornstarch and remaining water; add to the sauce and stir. Makes approximately 1 pint.

This sauce will keep up to 6 weeks in the refrigerator.

Variation: You can replace $1/3$ cup of the water with peach or pineapple juice. The juice gives the sauce an excellent taste.

Soups &
Stews

Cream of Asparagus Soup

4 tablespoons butter

6 green onions, sliced

2 tablespoons flour

$1/2$ teaspoon salt

$1/8$ teaspoon white pepper

3 cups chicken broth

2 (8-ounce) packages frozen asparagus

2 cups light cream

Croutons

Melt butter in large heavy-bottom saucepan or a 10-inch Dutch oven. Sauté onions until they turn transparent, about 5 or so minutes. Blend in flour, salt, and pepper. Add broth and bring to a boil. Add asparagus, cover loosely, and allow to simmer for about 20 minutes. Cool slightly and purée in a blender or food processor. Return to pan to reheat then add cream. Serve with croutons. Makes 6–8 servings.

Easy Cabbage Soup

1 pound lean ground beef

1 medium onion, chopped

$^1/_2$ cup chopped celery

1 (28-ounce) can stewed tomatoes, with liquid

2 cups shredded cabbage

2 (12-ounce) cans V-8 juice

1 (15-ounce) can kidney beans, with liquid

1 teaspoon chili powder or taco seasoning

In a large saucepan, brown the beef. Add the remaining ingredients and cook until cabbage is tender, about 10–15 minutes. Makes 8–10 servings.

Cabbage and Tomato Soup

2 quarts cold water

2 onions, chopped

2 bay leaves

1 tablespoon salt

2 tablespoons apple cider vinegar

2 tablespoons sugar

4 tomatoes, diced, or 2 cups canned diced tomatoes

2 heads cabbage, coarsely chopped

$1/2$ cup grated carrots

$1/2$ cup chopped celery

4 to 5 pounds soup bones, chicken parts, or inexpensive beef, or 4 to 5 beef and/or chicken bouillon cubes

Preheat kitchen oven to 320 degrees, or prepare 12–14 coals for cooking outside using a volcano stove, or 25 coals for cooking outside using Dutch oven.

Combine all ingredients in 12-inch Dutch oven. Bake for 45 minutes in your kitchen oven, use 12–14 coals in a volcano stove, or 10 coals on the bottom and 15 coals on the top of your Dutch oven and simmer until vegetables and meat are done. Makes 12 servings.

Zucchini Soup

2 medium zucchini, diced

2 teaspoons dry minced onion

1 clove garlic, minced

1 teaspoon butter

$^1/_4$ teaspoon celery salt

1 teaspoon curry powder

$^1/_2$ cup light cream or evaporated milk

1 (15-ounce) can chicken broth

In a large saucepan, sauté zucchini with onion and garlic in butter for about 5 minutes. Add celery salt and curry and simmer on a low heat, covered, for 15 minutes. Blend in blender or use hand mixer and then add cream and broth and blend until smooth. Serve hot or cold. Makes 2–4 servings.

Celery and Lentil Soup

1 ham bone or 1 cup chopped ham

2 quarts water

1 bay leaf

$1/4$ teaspoon garlic salt or powder

$1/4$ teaspoon oregano, optional

Salt and pepper, to taste

1 cup lentils

1 onion, chopped

1 stalk celery, chopped (leeks may be substituted)

Place ham bone, water, bay leaf, and seasonings in a large stockpot or 12-inch Dutch oven and simmer for 2 hours. Discard bone and bay leaf. Add lentils, onion, and celery. Simmer 1 hour more. Serve with crackers or cheesy biscuits. Makes 6–8 servings.

Hamburger and Vegetable Soup

1 pound ground beef

1 cup chopped onion

2 cups diced potatoes

2 cups shredded cabbage

1 $^1/_2$ cups sliced celery

4 cups whole canned tomatoes

$^1/_2$ cup uncooked white or brown rice

5 cups water

1 bay leaf

Salt and pepper, to taste

In a large stockpot, cook the beef and onion until meat is browned. Add remaining ingredients and cook for 1 hour or until vegetables are tender. Season with salt and pepper, to taste. Makes 8 servings.

Cooking variations: You can make this soup in a 12-inch Dutch oven using 9 coals on the bottom and 14 coals on the top for 1 hour or cook in a crock pot on high for 2 hours after browning the meat in a skillet.

Taco Soup

1/2 pound ground beef

1/2 pound ground sausage

1 medium onion, chopped

1 green bell pepper, chopped

1 red bell pepper, chopped

1/2 cup green onions, chopped, optional

1/2 cup celery, chopped, optional

2 quarts water

1 (2-ounce) package taco seasoning

12 (8-inch) round corn tortillas, cut into small pieces

Salt and pepper, to taste

Grated cheddar cheese

Sour cream

Sauté beef, sausage, onion, bell peppers, and celery in a 12-inch Dutch oven until cooked through on your kitchen stove or a camp stove. Add water and taco seasoning and simmer for 15 minutes. Add tortilla shells and simmer for another 15 minutes. Season with salt and pepper, to taste. Serve with grated cheese and sour cream. Makes 8–10 servings.

Variation: Omit 1 quart of water and add 1 quart of spaghetti sauce or add extra chili powder, to taste, for a spicier seasoning.

Easy Tortilla Soup

1 medium onion, chopped

4 garlic cloves, chopped

1 pound ground beef

$1/2$ pound ground sausage

2 (10.75-ounce) cans cream of chicken soup

2 (10.75-ounce) cans cream of celery soup

1 (10.75-ounce) can cheddar cheese soup

2 (15-ounce) cans chicken broth

1 (15-ounce) can diced Mexican-style tomatoes

$1/2$ cup medium salsa

1 (4.5-ounce) can green chiles

1 teaspoon chili powder

Salt and pepper, to taste

12 (8-inch) round corn tortillas

$1/2$ pound grated Colby Jack cheese

Sour cream

Chopped onions

Crushed tortilla chips or corn chips

Warm and lightly grease a 12-inch deep Dutch oven and sauté onions and garlic until translucent. Add beef and sausage and cook until browned. Remove meat mixture from Dutch oven and then pour the soups and broth into the Dutch oven and whisk until smooth. Add tomatoes, salsa, chiles, chili powder, salt, and pepper. Bring to a simmer then add meat mixture. Allow to simmer for 30 minutes on your kitchen stove top or a camp stove. While soup is simmering, cut tortillas into small, thin strips. Add to soup and continue to simmer for 10 more minutes.

To serve, ladle soup into a bowls. Top with cheese, sour cream, onions, and/ or crushed chips. Makes 10–12 servings.

German Potato Soup

8 cups cubed potatoes

1 $1/4$ cups sliced celery

$1/2$ cup chopped onion

6 cups water

$1/2$ teaspoon salt

$1/8$ teaspoon pepper

Drop Dumplings

1 egg, beaten

$1/2$ teaspoon salt

$1/3$ cup water

$3/4$ cup flour

Prepare 20 coals for cooking outside using a Dutch oven.

Combine soup ingredients in a 12-inch Dutch oven and cook until potatoes are tender, about 1 hour, using 8 coals on the bottom and 12 coals on the top of your Dutch oven. When the vegetables are tender, mash with a potato masher.

For the drop dumplings: combine egg, salt, water, and flour. Stir until smooth and stiff. Drop by teaspoonfuls onto hot soup. Cover with lid and place back on the coals for about 15 more minutes to cook dumplings. Do not lift lid during cooking time. The smell will tell you when it's done. Makes 6–8 servings.

Variation: 1 cup of cooked chopped ham or bacon can be added after mashing the vegetables for a meaty taste.

Cooking variation: This soup can also be made in a 6-quart stockpot on your kitchen stove.

Irish Stew

2 tablespoons vegetable oil

2 pounds stew beef or lamb, cut into 1-inch pieces

2 cups chopped onions

$1/2$ teaspoon salt

$1/4$ teaspoon pepper

1 (15-ounce) can beef broth

1 cup dark beer

1 pound potatoes, sliced and quartered

3 carrots, cut into $1/2$-inch pieces

2 tablespoons cornstarch

3 tablespoons water

Parsley

In a large stockpot, heat oil over medium heat. Add beef and onions and brown evenly, stirring occasionally. Pour off drippings. Return beef mixture to pot and season with salt and pepper. Stir in broth and beer. Bring to a slow rolling boil. Reduce heat to low, cover, and let simmer for 1 hour. Add potatoes and carrots. Bring to a boil and reduce heat to low. Allow to cook for 20–30 minutes until beef and vegetables are tender. Combine cornstarch with water and add to pot. Bring to a boil and cook until thickened. Garnish with chopped parsley. Makes 8–10 servings.

Cooking variations: You can make this stew in a 12-inch Dutch oven using 9 coals on the bottom and 15 coals on the top. Or, after browning the meat, place all ingredients in a slow cooker and cook on low for 4–5 hours.

Lenny's Stew

2 cups cooked beef, cut into 1-inch cubes

3 tablespoons vegetable oil

1 medium onion, chopped

1 medium green bell pepper, chopped

$1/4$ cup chopped celery

1 clove garlic, chopped

5 medium tomatoes, peeled and chopped, or 1 (28-ounce) can stewed tomatoes, with liquid

$1/4$ cup water

$1\,1/4$ teaspoons salt

1 tablespoon chili powder

1 teaspoon Worcestershire sauce

4 to 5 cups mashed potatoes, optional

Fry beef in hot oil in a large cast iron skillet until browned. Add onion, bell pepper, celery, and garlic; cook until tender. Add remaining ingredients; reduce to low heat and simmer for 20 minutes. Pour into serving dish and top with mashed potatoes, if desired. Makes 8–10 servings.

Variation: You can thicken the stew by dissolving 3 teaspoons of cornstarch in $1/4$ cup water and adding to mixture before topping with potatoes and serving.

Cooking variations: This stew can be cooked for 1 hour in a 12-inch Dutch oven using 10 coals on the bottom and 15 coals on the top. You can also place the Dutch oven in your kitchen oven at 300 degrees for 1 hour. The smell will make your mouth water.

Astoria Beef Stew

2 pounds lean stew meat, cut into small pieces

2 medium onions, cut in chunks

1 cup sliced celery

2 cups sliced carrots

4 potatoes, cut in lengthwise wedges

1 teaspoon salt

$^1/_2$ teaspoon pepper

3 tablespoons minute tapioca

1 (10.75-ounce) can tomato soup

1 soup can water

Prepare 22–25 coals for cooking outside using a Dutch oven. Warm and grease a 12-inch Dutch oven.

Place pieces of beef in Dutch oven and arrange vegetables around them in an attractive pattern. Sprinkle with salt, pepper, and tapioca. Combine soup and water together and pour over all ingredients in the Dutch oven. Cook, using 9 coals on the bottom and 13–15 coals on the top of your Dutch oven for 1 hour or until vegetables are tender. The smell will tell you when it is done. Makes 6–8 servings.

Cooking variation: You can also place the Dutch oven in your kitchen oven at 325 degrees for 1 hour, or until the smell is very strong.

Company Chicken Stew

4 cups chicken broth

2 cups water

1 tablespoon chicken flavoring or bouillon

1 bay leaf

Salt and pepper, to taste

$1/2$ teaspoon garlic pepper salt

1 teaspoon onion salt

2 cups cubed cooked chicken

1 cup green peas

1 cup diced carrots

1 cup diced celery

1 cup lima beans

4 to 5 cups mashed potatoes or rice

Warm and grease a 12-inch Dutch oven. Place liquids and seasonings inside. Bring to a simmer. Slowly add chicken and vegetables; simmer 5 minutes. Cover and simmer on very low heat until tender. This dish is usually done in less than a half hour. Serve with mashed potatoes or rice. Makes 8–10 servings.

Variation: If you wish to thicken the liquid, dissolve 3 tablespoons of cornstarch in $1/4$ cup water and add to the mixture. Simmer for another 5 minutes to thicken.

Main
Dishes

Bacon-Wrapped Chicken Breasts

2 tablespoons vegetable oil

1 medium onion, chopped

16 slices bacon

3 tablespoons garlic lemon pepper

$1/2$ cup flour

8 skinned chicken breasts

8 small red potatoes, cut in half

1 (1-pound) package small carrots

Preheat kitchen oven to 300 degrees or prepare 24 coals for cooking outside using a Dutch oven. Warm and grease the bottom of a 12-inch Dutch oven and warm and grease a 12-inch cast iron skillet.

Place the oil in the prepared Dutch oven and sauté the onion on your kitchen stove top or a camp stove. Lay 8 bacon slices across the bottom of the oven and turn off the heat.

Mix lemon pepper with flour in a pie pan. Rinse chicken breasts in cold water and roll in flour. On your stove top, brown the chicken on both sides in the prepared skillet and then place chicken on top of bacon in the Dutch oven. Brown the remaining slices of bacon in the skillet and lay across the top of the chicken. Spread the carrots and potatoes across the top of the chicken breasts. Bake for 50 minutes in your kitchen oven or use 9 coals on the bottom and 15 coals on the top of your Dutch oven. Makes 8 servings.

Baked Tomato Chicken

1 medium red onion, thinly sliced

8 chicken thighs

1 (15-ounce) can diced tomatoes with liquid

¹/₄ cup light balsamic vinaigrette dressing

¹/₄ teaspoon garlic powder

¹/₄ cup grated Parmesan cheese

Preheat kitchen oven to 300 degrees or prepare 21 coals for cooking outside using a Dutch oven. Warm and grease a 10-inch Dutch oven.

Place onion in bottom of Dutch oven and top with chicken. Combine tomatoes, dressing, and garlic powder; pour over chicken. Sprinkle with cheese.

Bake for 45 minutes in your kitchen oven or use 7 coals on the bottom and 14 coals on the top of your Dutch oven. The chicken should be cooked to 165 degrees. You will smell the chicken when it is done. Makes 8 servings.

Bedroll Chicken

6 skinless chicken breasts

Salt and pepper, to taste

1 teaspoon all-purpose seasoning

1 pound bacon

1 (16-ounce) package thinly sliced ham

6 slices white cheese, of choice, cut in half

12 ounces sour cream

$^1/_4$ cup water

1 (10.75-ounce) can cream of mushroom soup

1 pound fresh mushrooms, sliced

Preheat kitchen oven to 300 degrees or prepare 22–23 coals for cooking outside using a Dutch oven. Warm and grease a 12-inch Dutch oven.

Sprinkle chicken with salt and pepper and seasoning and cut each breast in half. Wrap slices of bacon around chicken pieces. Place pieces of ham on bottom of prepared Dutch oven. Place chicken pieces on top of ham and top with cheese slices. Combine sour cream, water, and soup and pour over top of chicken.

Bake for 35–45 minutes in your kitchen oven or use 8 coals on the bottom and 14–15 on the top of your Dutch oven. Add mushrooms about 10 minutes before serving. Makes 6 servings.

Cooking variation: If you use a propane camp stove, use very low heat and a deflector shield over the burner.

Chicken Legs, Thighs, and Celery

8 to 10 chicken legs and thighs

2 tablespoons vegetable oil

$1/2$ cup flour

1 (16-ounce) bottle French dressing

1 cup apricot-pineapple jam

1 (2-ounce) package dry onion soup mix

1 medium onion, sliced

6 to 8 celery ribs, thinly sliced

Prepare 22–28 coals for cooking outside using a Dutch oven. Warm and grease a 12-inch Dutch oven.

Coat chicken with flour and brown in prepared Dutch oven. Add dressing, jams, and soup mix. Place onion rings and celery on top. Cook for 1 hour using 8–10 coals on the bottom and 14–18 coals on the top of your Dutch oven. Serve with rice. Makes 8–10 servings.

Cooking variation: You can bake this in your kitchen oven at 300 degrees for 1 hour.

Chicken Tortilla Dinner

1/4 cup vegetable oil

1 medium onion, finely chopped

1 green bell pepper, chopped

1 red bell pepper, chopped

1 teaspoon garlic salt or powder

1 teaspoon all-purpose seasoning

2 cups diced cooked chicken

1 cup salsa

3 cups roasted garlic spaghetti sauce

3 cups cut-up corn tortillas

2 cups grated cheddar cheese

3 green onions, chopped

On your kitchen stove top, in a lightly warmed and greased 10-inch Dutch oven, place oil, onion, bell peppers, and seasonings. Sauté until onions are transparent. Add chicken, salsa, and spaghetti sauce. Bring to a slow boil and stir in tortilla pieces. Spread cheese on top and sprinkle green onions on cheese. Return to heat with a cover and let stand for 5 minutes before serving. Great served with green salad. Makes 4–6 servings.

Easy Apricot Chicken

1 medium onion, sliced

1 green bell pepper, sliced

6 boneless, skinless chicken breasts

1 (16-ounce) bottle Russian salad dressing

1 (12-ounce) jar apricot jam or marmalade

1 (2-ounce) package onion soup mix

Preheat kitchen oven to 300 degrees or prepare 23 coals for cooking outside using a Dutch oven. Warm and grease a 12-inch Dutch oven.

Place slices of onion and bell pepper on the bottom of the Dutch oven. Place chicken breasts on the vegetables. Mix remaining ingredients and pour over chicken. Cover and bake for 1 hour in your kitchen oven or use 8 coals on the bottom and 15 coals on the top of your Dutch oven. The cooking time should be the same. If the coals burn down because of wind, replace with new ones after 30 minutes. Makes 6 servings.

TIP: Dutch ovens are like a pressure cooker—they vent when they are done and out comes the smell. Do not lift the lid because you let out pressure, moisture, and heat. It will not burn if you keep your coals in a circle underneath.

Log Cabin Chicken Pie

Crust

- 2 cups flour
- 1 teaspoon salt
- $2/3$ cup lard or shortening
- 1 egg
- 1 tablespoon lemon juice, optional
- 2 to 3 tablespoons cold milk

Filling

- 1 $1/2$ cups chicken stock
- 3 tablespoons flour
- $1/4$ cup water
- 3 cups diced cooked chicken

Topping

- 1 $1/2$ cups bread crumbs
- 1 medium onion, finely chopped
- $1/2$ teaspoon salt
- $1/2$ teaspoon pepper
- $1/2$ cup finely chopped celery
- 1 $1/2$ cups chicken stock, warmed

Preheat kitchen oven to 350 degrees and warm and grease a 10-inch deep Dutch oven or Camp Chef cast iron pie pan.

To make the crust; sift together flour and salt in large bowl. Cut in lard until crumbs are pea-sized. In a small bowl, blend together the egg and lemon juice and toss with flour mix. Add milk and toss until moist enough to form ball. Roll dough out on floured board making 1 (10-inch) round pie crust and place in the Dutch oven or pie pan.

To make the filling; heat the chicken stock but do not boil. Add flour to the water and mix to a paste. Add to chicken stock, stirring constantly. When thickened, add the chicken and spoon into pie crust.

For the topping; combine bread crumbs with onion in a medium bowl. Add seasonings and celery. Add chicken stock and combine until moist. Spread over the filling. Bake for 40 minutes and serve. Makes 8–10 servings.

TIP: The less you handle pie crust, the better it is.

Fried Chicken Romano

3 tablespoons seasoned bread crumbs

3 tablespoons grated Romano cheese

6 boneless chicken breasts

1 $^1/_2$ tablespoons olive oil

1 (15-ounce) can diced tomatoes with Italian herbs, drained and liquid reserved

$^1/_2$ to $^3/_4$ teaspoon garlic salt

2 tablespoons sliced black olives

1 teaspoon vinegar

$^1/_8$ teaspoon cayenne pepper

3 tablespoons dried basil leaves

Combine bread crumbs and cheese in a large ziplock bag. Shake chicken breasts in crumb mix to coat both sides. Heat oil in a 10-inch Dutch oven on your kitchen stove top. Cook chicken until golden and cooked through, about 3–4 minutes each side.

In a small saucepan, combine tomatoes, garlic salt, olives, vinegar, pepper, and $^1/_3$ cup of the reserved tomato liquid. Cook for a couple of minutes, stirring occasionally, until slightly thickened. Remove from heat. Stir in basil. Spoon sauce over chicken and allow to simmer in covered Dutch oven for 10 minutes while the taste works through chicken. Makes 6 servings.

Stuffed Chicken Breast

1 chicken breast, scored halfway through

$1/8$ teaspoon salt

$1/8$ teaspoon pepper

1 tablespoon chopped onion

1 tablespoon chopped celery

1 tablespoon butter

$1/8$ teaspoon dried thyme

$1/8$ teaspoon dried basil

$1/8$ teaspoon parsley flakes

1 slice day-old white bread, cubed

2 tablespoons chicken broth

All-purpose seasoning, to taste

Preheat kitchen oven to 325 degrees. Warm and grease an 8-inch Dutch oven.

Sprinkle chicken with salt and pepper; set aside. In a small skillet, sauté onion and celery in butter until soft; stir in seasonings, bread, and broth. Place in cavity of chicken. Place in prepared Dutch oven. Sprinkle with all-purpose seasoning. Bake for 45 minutes. Makes 1 serving.

Note: To feed a lot of people, simply prepare one piece per person and use a Dutch oven large enough to hold the chicken. This is an easy dish to do for company.

Stuffed Chicken Supper

2 tablespoons butter

1 large onion, chopped

1 cup sliced mushrooms

$1/2$ cup diced and cooked bacon

$1/2$ teaspoon parsley

$1/2$ teaspoon sage

Salt and pepper, to taste

6 red potatoes, cubed

1 egg

1 (3-pound) whole roasting chicken

4 ounces chicken stock

Preheat kitchen oven to 325 degrees or prepare 25 coals for cooking outside using a Dutch oven.

Make stuffing by lightly frying butter, onion, mushrooms, and bacon in a 10-inch cast iron skillet. Add seasoning and potatoes and mix in the egg.

Wash and dry chicken. Spoon stuffing mixture into chicken cavity and then place in a 12-inch Dutch oven. Carefully pour the stock around the chicken. Bake for $1 1/2$ hours or until juices run clear. If you are cooking outside, use 10 coals on the bottom and 15 coals on the top of your Dutch oven. You most likely will need to replace the coals after 45 minutes to maintain your baking temperature. You will smell it when it's done. Makes 6–8 servings.

Variations: Sprinkle one teaspoon of all-purpose seasoning on top of chicken for color and flavor. Extra red potatoes can be placed in the oven with small carrots for extra company.

Pork Chops

4 to 6 pork chops

1 (10.75-ounce) can cream of celery soup

1 medium onion, chopped

$^1/_2$ cup water

Salt and pepper, to taste

Preheat kitchen oven to 300 degrees or prepare 20–26 coals for cooking outside using a Dutch oven. Warm and grease a 12-inch Dutch oven.

On your stove top, brown chops in prepared Dutch oven. Add soup, onion, water, and salt and pepper, to taste. Bake for 1 hour in your kitchen oven or use 6–8 coals on the bottom and 14–18 coals on the top of your Dutch oven. The smell will tell you when it's done. Serve with mashed potatoes or twice baked potatoes and a side dish of green beans. Makes 4–6 servings.

Pork Chops
from the South

6 pork chops

2 tablespoons vegetable oil

1 medium onion, sliced

$1/4$ cup creamy peanut butter

$1/2$ (10.75-ounce) can cream of mushroom soup

$1/3$ cup milk

1 teaspoon Worcestershire sauce, optional

1 teaspoon salt

$1/8$ teaspoon pepper

Preheat kitchen oven to 300 degrees.

In a 12-inch cast iron skillet, brown pork chops quickly on both sides in oil. Top each pork chop with an onion slice. Mix remaining ingredients together and spoon over pork chops. Cover and bake for 30–45 minutes. The smell will tell you when it is ready. The chops will be very tender and are tasty served over rice or mashed potatoes. Makes 6 servings.

Cooking variation: This recipe can also be prepared in a 12-inch Dutch oven and cooked outside using 9 coals on the bottom and 15 coals on the top.

Bunkhouse Pork Chops

¹/₄ cup flour

6 pork chops

2 tablespoons vegetable oil

1 cup water

1 (10.75-ounce) can cream of mushroom soup

2 tablespoons packed brown sugar

1 medium onion, chopped

1 teaspoon garlic powder

3 tablespoons ketchup

¹/₄ cup sour cream

Lightly flour pork chops and brown in a large skillet with 2 tablespoons oil. Place chops, water, soup, brown sugar, and onion in a 12-inch warmed and greased Dutch oven. Cover and simmer for 30 minutes. Be sure to scrape all drippings from the pan into the Dutch oven. Sprinkle with garlic powder and ketchup. You can simmer on the stove top over very low heat or outside over 10 coals.

If sauce is not thick enough, dissolve 2 heaping tablespoons of flour into ¹/₄ cup warm water and gradually add to the Dutch oven. While adding flour mixture, stir constantly to keep from lumping. When consistency is how you want it, stir in sour cream and heat thoroughly without boiling. Chops will be very tender. The smell will be to die for. Makes 6 servings.

Fiesta Pork Chops

6 loin pork chops

1 (3-ounce) package dry onion soup mix

Pepper, to taste

2 tablespoons vegetable oil

$3/4$ cup uncooked long grain rice

1 $1/2$ cups water

1 (8-ounce) can tomato sauce

$1/4$ cup taco seasoning mix

1 medium green bell pepper, chopped

$1/2$ cup grated cheddar cheese

Preheat kitchen oven to 300 degrees.

Season pork chops with soup mix and pepper. Place in a 12-inch Dutch oven and brown both sides of chops in oil.

In a medium bowl, combine rice, water, tomato sauce, and taco seasoning and mix well. Pour mixture over the pork chops and top with bell pepper. Cover and bake for 1 $1/2$ hours. Uncover and sprinkle with cheese. Cover until cheese is melted. This is an excellent dish and chops remain moist. Makes 6 servings.

Easy Pork Roast

$^1/_4$ cup vegetable oil

1 medium onion, sliced

1 (4- to 5-pound) bone-in pork roast

1 (3-ounce) package dry onion soup mix

1 (10.75-ounce) can cream of mushroom soup

1 teaspoon thyme

$^1/_2$ teaspoon sage

$^1/_4$ cup milk

2 cups sliced carrots, optional

2 cups sliced potatoes, optional

$^1/_2$ cup sliced celery, optional

Preheat kitchen oven to 325 degrees. Warm a 12-inch Dutch oven.

Pour oil into prepared Dutch oven. Scatter onion on the bottom and place roast on top.

In a small bowl, combine soups, thyme, sage, and milk. Pour mixture on top of the pork roast. Place lid on the Dutch oven and bake for 1 $^1/_2$ hours or until the meat fall off the bones if you are not using the vegetables.

If you are using the vegetables, remove the roast from oven after 1 hour and place carrots, potatoes, and celery around it. Return to the oven and bake for 30 minutes. The smell will tell you when it is ready. Makes 8–10 servings.

Ham and Chicken Soup

3 tablespoons chopped onion

$1/4$ cup chopped green bell pepper

$1/4$ cup butter

6 tablespoons flour

2 cups milk

2 cups diced cooked ham

1 (10.75-ounce) can cream of chicken soup

Preheat kitchen oven to 340 degrees.

Sauté onion and bell pepper in butter in a 10-inch cast iron skillet until tender. Blend in flour. Add milk, ham, and soup. Boil for 1 minute, stirring constantly. Bake until mixture thickens, about 45 minutes. Makes 4 servings.

Variation: To make this what my grandmother called a "soup pie," top with prepared cornbread mix and bake an additional 15 minutes.

Porky Pineapple Spare Ribs

¹/₂ cup flour

1 teaspoon salt

¹/₄ teaspoon pepper

4 pounds boneless pork spareribs

¹/₂ cup bacon grease or shortening, melted

1 (16-ounce) can pineapple tidbits, drained and liquid reserved

¹/₄ cup apple cider vinegar

¹/₂ cup ketchup

¹/₄ cup molasses

1 large onion, finely chopped

1 large green bell pepper, chopped

Preheat kitchen oven to 325 degrees or prepare 25 coals for cooking outside using a Dutch oven. Warm and grease a 12-inch Dutch oven.

Combine flour, salt, and pepper on a plate and roll ribs in mixture. Brown ribs in grease in prepared Dutch oven. Remove from grease and place on paper towels to drain.

Place reserved pineapple juice and vinegar in Dutch oven and simmer until bubbling with the leftover oils. Put the ribs back into the oven. Cover and cook in your kitchen oven for 30 minutes or use 10 coals on the bottom and 15 coals on the top of your Dutch oven.

Remove lid and stir ribs to baste with juices. Add ketchup and molasses and cook until ribs are tender, another 10–20 minutes. Add pineapple chunks, onion, and bell pepper. Put back on heat for 10 minutes to heat through. Excellent served with rice. Makes 8–10 servings.

Rum Baked Ham

1 (3- to 4-pound) boneless smoked ham
Whole cloves
2 cloves garlic, mashed
1 tablespoon Dijon mustard
1/2 cup chili sauce
3/4 cup packed brown sugar
1 tablespoon dark rum flavoring
1 medium onion, sliced

Preheat kitchen oven to 325 degrees or prepare 25 coals for cooking outside using a Dutch oven. Warm and grease a 12-inch Dutch oven.

With sharp knife, score top of ham in a diamond pattern. Stud with cloves at every score.

Combine garlic, mustard, chili sauce, brown sugar, and rum in small bowl; mix well. Spread evenly over top and sides of ham. Place onion slices on the bottom of Dutch oven and place ham inside. Bake for 1 hour in your kitchen oven or use 10 coals on the bottom and 15 coals on the top of your Dutch oven. The smell will let you know when it is done. Makes 8–10 servings.

Variation: If you want more flavor, put 2 to 3 slices of green bell pepper beside ham when you start cooking.

Celery and Ham Loaf

1 1/2 pounds chopped ham

1/2 pound ground pork

2 eggs, slightly beaten

1/2 cup milk

1 cup soft bread crumbs

1 teaspoon prepared mustard

1 medium onion, chopped

1/2 cup chopped celery

1/8 teaspoon pepper

Preheat kitchen oven to 325 degrees. Warm and grease a 10-inch Dutch oven.

Combine all ingredients in a large bowl and mix well. Press lightly into prepared Dutch oven and bake for 1 hour. Serve with fried potatoes and corn. Makes 8 servings.

TIP: This can be used as a breakfast meat, too.

Campfire Mushroom Burgers

2 pounds ground beef

3 medium onions, chopped

1 (10.75-ounce) can cream of mushroom soup

2 cups sliced mushrooms, canned or fresh

$1/8$ teaspoon nutmeg

Salt and pepper, to taste

8 hamburger buns

Sliced onion, optional

Sauté beef and onions in a large skillet over 14–16 coals or on a Camp Chef propane camp stove. Stir to break meat into small pieces. Add soup, mushrooms, and seasonings. Simmer for 3–4 minutes while you place the bread on plates. You can put a fresh slice of onion on the bread before spooning the mixture over the top, if desired. Makes 8 servings.

Variations: Add chopped olives, red or green bell peppers, sliced tomatoes, stewed tomatoes, green chiles, grated cheese, or use your imagination to create a great sandwich.

Hamburger Cabbage Rolls

1 medium head cabbage

Boiling water

$3/4$ cup leftover cooked rice

1 pound ground beef

$1/4$ pound country sausage

3 teaspoons chopped green onion

$1/4$ teaspoon garlic salt

$1/4$ cup minced celery

1 egg, beaten

$1/2$ cup milk

1 teaspoon salt

$1/2$ cup water

Preheat kitchen oven to 300 degrees or prepare 23–24 coals for cooking outside using a Dutch oven. Warm and grease a 12-inch Dutch oven.

Trim off soiled cabbage leaves and remove core. Place in a large bowl and pour boiling water over the cabbage and let stand for 4–5 minutes, until leaves are limp. Select largest ones for rolls.

Combine remaining ingredients except for water in a large bowl. Roll about $1/2$ cup of this mixture in individual cabbage leaves and fasten with toothpicks. Lay flap side down in prepared Dutch oven, add water, and cover with remaining cabbage leaves. Place the lid on the Dutch oven. Simmer in kitchen oven for 45 minutes or use 9 coals on the bottom and 14–15 coals on the top of your Dutch oven. The smell will tell you when it is done. Makes 7–8 servings.

Enchilada Hamburger Pie

1 pound ground beef

¹/₂ pound country sausage

1 large onion, chopped

2 tablespoons vegetable oil

1 (10.75-ounce) can cream of mushroom soup

1 (10.75-ounce) can cream of chicken soup

1 (15-ounce) can enchilada sauce

1 cup milk

¹/₂ teaspoon chili powder

¹/₄ teaspoon garlic powder

¹/₂ teaspoon onion salt

1 dozen corn tortillas cut into strips

¹/₂ pound grated cheddar cheese

¹/₄ cup chopped green onions

Preheat kitchen oven to 300 degrees or prepare 21 coals for cooking outside using a Dutch oven. Warm and grease a 10-inch Dutch oven.

On the stove top, brown beef, sausage, and onion in oil in prepared Dutch oven; add soups, sauce, milk, and seasonings. Spoon out ¹/₂ the mixture into a bowl and set aside.

Top remaining meat mixture in Dutch oven with ¹/₂ of the tortilla strips, followed by ¹/₂ of the reserved meat mixture, repeat with meat as the last layer. Top with cheese and green onions. Bake for about 45 minutes in your kitchen oven or use 8 coals on the bottom and 13 coals on the top of your Dutch oven. The smell will tell you when it's done. Makes 8–10 servings.

Mushroom Steak

6 (6- to 8-ounce) cubed steaks

$1/4$ cup vegetable oil

$1/4$ cup flour

$1/2$ cup water

1 (10.75-ounce) can cream of mushroom soup

1 (6-ounce) can whole or sliced mushrooms

2 large onions, chopped

4 medium potatoes, diced

4 large carrots, thinly sliced

3 celery ribs, chopped

1 teaspoon all-purpose seasoning

Salt and pepper, to taste

Preheat kitchen oven to 325 degrees. Warm and grease a 12-inch Dutch oven.

Place steak in prepared Dutch oven. Add the oil and flour. Stir and brown meat. Add the water and soup. Add the mushrooms, onions, and remaining vegetables. Sprinkle with all-purpose seasoning and salt and pepper. Cover and bake in your kitchen oven for about 1 1/2 hours. Makes 6 servings.

Dutch Oven Pepper Steak

2 to 3 pounds round or top sirloin steak

1 cup flour

1 teaspoon salt

$^1/_2$ teaspoon pepper

$^1/_2$ teaspoon garlic powder

$^1/_4$ cup plus 2 tablespoons vegetable oil, divided

$^1/_2$ large onion, sliced

$^1/_2$ large onion, chopped

$^1/_2$ red onion, sliced

Water

1 (16-ounce) can brown gravy with mushrooms

1 (3-ounce) package dry onion soup mix

1 each red and yellow bell peppers, sliced

1 Anaheim pepper, sliced

$^3/_4$ to 1 pound fresh mushrooms, sliced

Prepare 40 coals for cooking outside using a Dutch oven.

Cut steak into serving sizes, 6–8 ounces per person. Combine the flour, salt, pepper, and garlic powder. Lightly coat meat with the flour mixture. Heat $^1/_4$ cup oil in 12-inch Dutch oven over 15 coals or use a propane camp stove. Brown floured steaks, remove, and discard oil. Place onions in Dutch oven with remaining oil and sauté for 2 minutes, top with steak, and add enough water to just cover the meat. Add gravy and onion soup mix. Simmer for 30–45 minutes or until tender using 10 coals on the bottom and 15 coals on the top of your Dutch oven. Add peppers and mushrooms to the meat and simmer until the peppers and mushrooms are soft. This will take about 20 minutes more. Makes 6–8 servings.

Quick-and-Easy Roast

1 onion, sliced

$^1/_4$ cup coffee

1 (4-pound) beef roast

1 (3-ounce) package dry onion soup mix

Preheat kitchen oven to 325 degrees and warm and grease a 12-inch Dutch oven.

Place the onion in the bottom of the prepared Dutch oven and pour in the coffee. Season roast with onion soup mix and place on top of the onions. Bake for about 2 hours. The smell will tell you when it is done. Makes 8–10 servings.

TIP: Your Dutch oven will tenderize the beef and break down the protein while maintaining almost all of the nutrients in your meat if you do not lift your lid.

Dutch Oven Pot Roast Dinner

2 tablespoons vegetable oil

1 medium onion, sliced, divided

1 (4- to 5-pound) pot roast

1 to 2 (10.75-ounce) cans cream of mushroom soup

6 to 8 potatoes, washed and quartered

10 to 12 carrots, peeled and cut

$^1/_2$ can water

Preheat kitchen oven to 300 degrees or prepare 50 coals for cooking outside using a Dutch oven. Warm a 12-inch Dutch oven.

Pour oil in the prepared Dutch oven and spread most of the onion on the bottom. Place meat on onion and add remaining onion to the top of the meat. Add soup, vegetables, and water. Cover and cook for 2–2 1/2 hours in your kitchen oven or use 10 coals on the bottom and 15 coals on the top of your Dutch oven. You will need to replace the coals after the first hour of cooking. Makes 10–12 servings.

Cooking variation: The recipe can be prepared on the stove top. If you simmer it on the stove, check it after an hour to make sure the moisture is sufficient to cover the vegetables. If low on moisture, add a little coffee or beef broth.

Standard Meat Loaf

1 egg

1 cup milk, or diluted gravy or tomato juice

1 pound ground beef

$1/2$ cup rolled oats or cracker crumbs

2 tablespoons finely chopped onion

1 teaspoon salt

$1/2$ teaspoon pepper

$1/2$ teaspoon sage

1 teaspoon dry mustard

1 tablespoon Worcestershire sauce

Preheat kitchen oven to 325 degrees.

In a large bowl, beat egg with milk and add meat along with the remaining ingredients. Mix well. Pack lightly in loaf pan, or be creative and make individual loaves in a muffin tin. Bake for 1 hour. If using muffin tins, check after 35 minutes for doneness. The smell will tell you when it is done. Makes 6–8 servings.

Country Balls of Meat

2/3 cup milk

1 egg

1 teaspoon salt

1/4 teaspoon pepper

1/4 teaspoon allspice

1/8 teaspoon cloves

1/2 cup cooked rice

1/2 cup bread crumbs

1/2 cup finely minced onion

1 pound ground beef

3 tablespoons vegetable oil

2 cups country gravy, spaghetti sauce, or brown mushroom gravy

1 cup sour cream

In a large bowl, combine milk, egg, and seasonings. Beat well. Stir in rice and bread crumbs. Add onion and beef; mix thoroughly. Form into 1 1/2-inch size balls.

Add oil to a 12-inch Dutch oven and heat. Place meat balls in the oil and slowly brown over medium heat. Turn the balls 2 or 3 times to cook through. Add country gravy, spaghetti sauce, or brown mushroom gravy. Heat through and serve over rice, potatoes, or cooked pasta. Makes 8–10 servings.

Veggie Garden Meatballs

1 pound ground beef

1 cup grated potato

2 eggs

2 cups grated carrots

1 medium onion, chopped

2$^1/_2$ cups crumbled corn flakes or crackers

$^1/_2$ teaspoon garlic salt

$^1/_2$ teaspoon celery salt

$^1/_2$ teaspoon salt

1 teaspoon pepper

1 (10.75-ounce) can cream of mushroom soup

$^1/_2$ cup milk

Preheat kitchen oven to 300 degrees.

In a large bowl, combine beef, potato, eggs, carrots, onion, corn flakes, and seasonings and mix well. Divide into 30 meatballs and brown in a 12-inch lightly greased Dutch oven. Combine soup and milk and pour over meatballs. Cover and bake for about an hour. The smell will tell you when it is done. These are good served with fresh green beans or corn and rolls. Makes 10 servings.

Utah Barbecued Meat

5 to 7 pounds beef or pork ribs

2 cups ketchup

2 teaspoons chili powder

2 tablespoons liquid smoke

$^1/_2$ cup Worcestershire sauce

$^1/_2$ cup lemon juice

2 teaspoons celery seed

2 cups water

2 teaspoons salt

Preheat kitchen oven to 300 degrees or prepare 75 coals for cooking outside using a Dutch oven. Warm and grease a 12-inch Dutch oven.

Brown the meat on your barbecue grill and then place meat in prepared Dutch oven. Combine the remaining ingredients in a large bowl and pour over the meat. Bake for 2–3 hours or until tender in your kitchen oven or use 8 coals on the bottom and 17 coals on the top of your Dutch oven. When cooking outside on coals, you will need to replace the coals about every 40 minutes, or 3 times. Open lid and baste twice during cooking time. Makes 10–14 servings.

TIP: It is important to cook this recipe slowly with a lower temperature so you don't dry out your meat.

Country Kitchen Casserole

6 slices bacon, diced

1 pound ground beef

$1/2$ pound sausage

1 cup chopped onions

$1/2$ teaspoon garlic salt

Salt and pepper, to taste

2 cups grated carrots

6 thinly sliced potatoes

$1/4$ cup Miracle Whip

1 (12-ounce) can tomato sauce

Preheat kitchen oven to 300 degrees or prepare 25 coals for cooking outside using a Dutch oven. Warm and grease a 12-inch Dutch oven.

Fry bacon until crisp in prepared Dutch oven. Add beef, sausage, and onions and cook only until red is gone from the meat. Season with garlic salt, salt, and pepper. Top with carrots and potatoes. Combine Miracle Whip and tomato sauce; pour over meat. Cover and cook for 35–45 minutes in your kitchen oven or use 10 coals on the bottom and 15 on the top of your Dutch oven. You will know it is done when you can smell it. Makes 8–10 servings.

Broccoli, Chicken, and Rice Casserole

3 cups chopped fresh broccoli

$1/2$ cup grated Parmesan cheese, divided

2 cups diced cooked chicken

1 cup cooked rice

2 tablespoons butter

2 tablespoons flour

1 cup milk

1 tablespoon lemon juice

8 ounces sour cream

Preheat kitchen oven to 300 degrees and grease a 10-inch Dutch oven.

Arrange broccoli in prepared Dutch oven. Sprinkle with half the cheese. Top with chicken and cover with rice.

In a small sauce pan, melt the butter and add flour. Add milk and slowly cook until bubbly. Remove from heat and add lemon juice and sour cream. Pour evenly over ingredients in the Dutch oven. Top with remaining cheese. Cover and bake for 20 minutes. You will get a great smell when it is done. Makes 4–6 servings.

Chinese Hamburger Casserole

- **1 pound ground beef**
- **1 medium onion, chopped**
- **3/4 cup celery, sliced diagonally**
- **1 (10-ounce) can water chestnuts, drained and chopped**
- **2 tablespoons soy sauce**
- **1 (10.75-ounce) can cream of mushroom soup**
- **1 cup Chinese noodles**

Preheat kitchen oven to 325 degrees. Warm and grease a 12-inch Dutch oven.

Brown beef with onion in prepared Dutch oven. Add celery, water chestnuts, soy sauce, and soup. Sprinkle noodles over the top of the hamburger mixture. Place lid on Dutch oven and bake for 25 minutes. Serve with white or brown cooked rice. Makes 4–6 servings.

Chili Corn Chip Casserole

1 pound sausage

1 pound ground beef

1 large onion, chopped

$^1/_2$ cup chopped celery

1 (15-ounce) can black beans

1 (15-ounce) can pinto beans

1 (15-ounce) can Mexican-style chili beans

$^1/_2$ teaspoon seasoned salt

$^1/_2$ teaspoon chili powder

3 cups corn chips, crushed, divided

1 $^1/_4$ cups grated cheddar cheese, divided

1 (18-ounce) can sliced black olives

Preheat kitchen oven to 325 or prepare 25 coals for cooking outside using a Dutch oven. Warm and lightly grease a 12-inch Dutch oven.

Add meats, onion, and celery to a large cast iron skillet. Cook until tender on low heat on kitchen stove top, about 4–5 minutes. Add beans, salt, and chili powder.

Place a layer of chips on the bottom of the prepared Dutch oven. Alternate layers of chips, cheese, and bean mixture, reserving $^1/_2$ cup of chips and $^1/_4$ cup of cheese for garnish. Top with olives. Bake for 25–30 minutes in your kitchen oven or use 10 coals on the bottom and 15 coals on the top of your Dutch oven. The smell will tell you when it's ready to eat. Makes 12–15 servings.

Olé Casserole

2 pounds ground beef

1 onion, chopped

1 green bell pepper, chopped

1 (29-ounce) can tomato sauce

1 (3-ounce) package taco seasoning

15 to 18 corn tortillas

1 (15-ounce) can kidney beans

2 cups grated cheddar cheese

1 (6-ounce) can sliced black olives

Cottage cheese

Sour cream

Preheat kitchen oven to 325 degrees or prepare 25 coals for cooking outside using a Dutch oven. Warm and grease a 12-inch Dutch oven.

Brown beef, onion, and bell pepper in a warmed and greased cast iron skillet. Add tomato sauce and taco seasoning and mix well. Set meat mixture aside.

In prepared Dutch oven, place layer of corn tortillas then beans, meat mixture, cheese, and olives. Bake for 20–30 minutes in your kitchen oven or use 10 coals on the bottom and 15 coals on the top of your Dutch oven. Serve with cottage cheese and sour cream. Makes 10–12 servings.

TIP: If your Dutch oven has legs, place it on a baking sheet or pizza pan to even the weight on the oven rack.

Enchilada Casserole

1 (16-ounce) can whole kernel corn

1 red bell pepper, chopped

1 green bell pepper, chopped

1 (16-ounce) can enchilada sauce

2 (10.75-ounce) cans cream of mushroom soup

8 to 10 beef or cheese enchiladas (see recipe below)

1 cup grated cheddar cheese

1 (10-ounce) bag corn or tortilla chips

Preheat kitchen oven to 300 degrees.

Combine corn, peppers, sauce, and soup in a 10-inch Dutch oven. Place enchiladas on top of soup mix. Sprinkle with cheese and cover with chips. Bake for 25–30 minutes. Makes 8–10 servings.

Enchiladas

1 pound ground beef

1 medium onion, chopped

Salt and pepper, to taste

8 to 10 corn tortillas

Brown beef and onions in a large skillet; add salt and pepper. Wrap mix in corn tortillas and use as directed above.

Sausage and Egg Casserole

1 pound cooked link sausages

2^1/$_2$ cups country gravy*

^{1}/$_2$ teaspoon sage

^{1}/$_2$ pound cheddar cheese, cubed

1 (8-ounce) can button mushrooms, drained

8 hard-boiled eggs, cut in half

Preheat kitchen oven to 325 degrees or prepare 21 coals for cooking outside using a Dutch oven. Warm and grease a 10-inch Dutch oven.

Cut sausages in half. Warm gravy in prepared Dutch oven and season with sage. Fold in sausages, cheese, and mushrooms. Press eggs into sausage mixture. Bake for 30–45 minutes in your kitchen oven or use 8 coals on the bottom and 13 coals on the top of your Dutch oven. Wait for the smell. Makes 8 servings.

*1 (3-ounce) package country gravy mix, prepared, will also equal this amount.

Crab Casserole

1 ¹/₂ cups crabmeat

6 hard-boiled eggs, chopped

1 ¹/₂ cups mayonnaise

1 cup heavy cream

1 tablespoon chopped parsley

1 teaspoon onion salt

¹/₄ teaspoon salt

¹/₈ teaspoon pepper

1 cup crushed Ritz crackers

Preheat kitchen oven to 300 degrees. Warm and grease a 10-inch Dutch oven.

In a large bowl, mix all ingredients except crackers and place in prepared Dutch oven. Top with the crackers. Bake for 45 minutes. Makes 6–8 servings.

Variation: You can substitute crushed corn flakes or buttered bread crumbs for the crackers.

Salmon and Rice Casserole Deluxe

1 cup chopped cooked salmon

2$^1/_2$ cups cooked rice

3 tablespoons butter

3 tablespoons flour

$^3/_4$ cup light cream

$^1/_2$ teaspoon paprika

$^3/_4$ teaspoon salt

$^1/_8$ teaspoon pepper

$^1/_8$ teaspoon minced garlic

1 teaspoon minced onion

$^1/_2$ cup grated white cheese, Monterey Jack, provolone or mozzarella

Preheat kitchen oven to 300 degrees or prepare 22–24 coals for cooking outside using a Dutch oven. Warm and grease a 10-inch Dutch oven.

Combine salmon with rice in a medium bowl and set aside.

Melt butter in a medium saucepan and blend in flour. Stir in cream and seasonings. Cook until thickened. This will make a white sauce.

Combine sauce and rice mixture in prepared Dutch oven. Sprinkle on minced onion and top with cheese. Cover and bake for 30 minutes in your kitchen oven or use 8–9 coals on the bottom and 14–15 coals on the top of your Dutch oven. Wait for the smell and enjoy. Makes 4 servings.

Cheesy One-Pot Skillet Meal

1 pound lean ground beef

¹/₂ pound country sausage

1 cup chopped onions

1 cup thinly sliced carrots

1 cup finely chopped potatoes

1 cup water

1 (15-ounce) can kidney beans, drained

¹/₂ cup barbecue sauce

1 cup grated cheddar cheese

Brown meat and onions in a 12-inch warmed and greased cast iron skillet on medium heat. Add vegetables; stir in water. Reduce heat to low; cover and simmer 15 minutes or until vegetables are tender. Add beans and barbecue sauce; stir. Cook 5 minutes or until heated through. Sprinkle with cheese. Easy and fast stove top meal. Makes 4–6 servings

Stroganoff in a Skillet

2 tablespoons flour

1 1/4 teaspoons salt, divided

1/8 teaspoon pepper

2 pounds sirloin steak, thinly sliced

2 tablespoons vegetable oil

1 cup chopped onion

1 clove garlic, minced

1 teaspoon Worcestershire sauce

**1 (10.75-ounce) can cream of chicken
or cream of mushroom soup**

1 cup sour cream

1/2 pound sliced mushrooms

1 1/3 cups beef bouillon broth

1 1/3 cups uncooked minute rice

Combine flour, 3/4 teaspoon salt, and pepper on a plate and coat steak pieces with flour mixture. Quickly brown meat in oil in a 12-inch cast iron skillet. Add onion and garlic and sauté until light brown; set aside.

In a large saucepan, combine Worcestershire sauce, soup, and sour cream and bring to a slow boil. Add remaining salt, mushrooms, broth, and rice.

Make a well in the center of the meat mixture and pour in the rice mixture. Stir gently enough to mix. Bring to a slow moving boil. Cover and let simmer for about 5 minutes or until rice is tender. Makes 6–8 servings.

Chili-Cheese Bites

$1/2$ pound ground beef

1 medium onion, chopped

1 teaspoon salt

$1/8$ teaspoon pepper

$1/2$ teaspoon chili powder

1 cup diced stewed tomatoes, divided

$1/4$ pound cheddar cheese, cubed

2 tablespoons vegetable oil

1 (20-ounce) can chili with beans

6 split hamburger or hot dog buns

$1/2$ cup ketchup

Grated cheddar cheese, optional

Combine beef, onion, salt, pepper, and chili powder in a large bowl. Add $1/2$ cup of diced tomatoes. Form balls around cubed cheese. Cook in 10-inch skillet with oil until browned. Add beans and remaining tomatoes. Simmer, uncovered for 4–5 minutes on a low heat.

Toast buns. Arrange meatballs on buns and cover with sauce and a spoonful of ketchup. You can top with a teaspoon full of grated cheddar cheese, if you like. Makes 6 servings.

Tamale Pie
for Company

2 large onions, finely chopped

1 clove garlic, minced

1 tablespoon olive oil

1 pound ground beef

1 tablespoon chili powder

$1/2$ teaspoon crushed basil leaves

$1/2$ teaspoon oregano

2 (10.75-ounce) cans tomato soup

1 (15-ounce) can kidney beans, drained

$2/3$ cup whole kernel corn

1 (16-ounce) package corn muffin mix*

$2/3$ cup milk

1 egg

Preheat kitchen oven to 325 degrees or prepare 21 coals for cooking outside using a Dutch oven.

Sauté onions and garlic in oil in a 10-inch Dutch oven. Add beef, chili powder, basil, and oregano and cook until onions are tender and meat is cooked. Stir in soup, beans, and corn and continue to cook until hot. Top with prepared corn muffin mix. Bake for 30 minutes in your kitchen oven or use 8 coals on the bottom and 13 coals on the top of your Dutch oven. Makes 6–8 servings.

*In a medium bowl, mix corn muffin mix, egg, and milk according to package directions until just combined. Mixture will be a little lumpy.

Easy Shepherd's Pie

1 pound ground beef

$1/2$ cup chopped onion

1 teaspoon garlic-pepper salt

1 (10.75-ounce) can tomato soup

1 (15-ounce) can green beans, drained

2 cups leftover mashed potatoes

$1/2$ cup grated cheddar-jack cheese

Preheat kitchen oven to 325 or prepare 22 coals for cooking outside using a Dutch oven.

Brown beef and onion in a 10-inch Dutch oven. Add garlic-pepper salt and soup and stir in green beans. Top with mashed potatoes and cheese. Bake for 30 minutes or until hot and the cheese melts in your kitchen oven or use 7 coals on the bottom and 15 coals on the top of your Dutch oven. Makes 6–8 servings.

Chuck Wagon Surprise

2 (10-count) cans refrigerator biscuits

$^1/_2$ cup grated cheddar-jack cheese

4 tablespoons mayonnaise

1 cup cut-up cooked chicken or pheasant, grouse, quail, or any bird desired

1 cup diced celery

1 tablespoon melted butter

Preheat kitchen oven to 325 degrees or prepare 24–25 coals for cooking outside using a Dutch oven. Grease a baking sheet or warm and grease a 12-inch Dutch oven.

Flatten 10 biscuits into a thin oval and place them on the prepared baking sheet or in the bottom of the prepared Dutch oven. Mix everything else together except the melted butter and spoon over the biscuits. Flatten and place remaining biscuits on top of the mixture and press edges together, if you so desire. Brush the melted butter on top and bake for 20–25 minutes in your kitchen oven or use 8 coals on the bottom and 16–17 coals on the top of your Dutch oven. Watch and wait for the smell. Makes 8–10 servings.

"If you ain't in a good mood when you cook these, you will be when you eat 'em."

On the trail, the cook used to sit on the chuck wagon seat and shoot prairie chicken, pheasant, or grouse and then fix what he shot for dinner for the men. The surprise came when the men bit into these biscuits because they didn't know what would be inside.

Foil Dinner for Scouts

4 tablespoons butter

1 pound ground beef, shaped into 4 patties

1 large onion, sliced

4 potatoes, quartered

1 celery rib, thinly sliced

4 slices tomato

4 carrots, thinly sliced

Salt and pepper, to taste

Tear 4 pieces of heavy-duty aluminum foil large enough to enclose hamburger patty and vegetables. Spread each piece of foil with 1 tablespoon of butter. Place hamburger patty on each piece of foil; add a slice of onion. Place quartered potato on onion slice; add celery, tomatoes, and carrots. Season with salt and pepper. Pull foil together and fold at top. Double wrap the foil dinner. Bake for 15–20 minutes over a camp fire on a grill or hot rock, turning often. The smell will tell you when it's done.

Serve immediately by sliding meat and vegetables out of the foil and on to a plate or eat from foil package. This is a great camp fire meal, because each person is responsible for their own meal—especially kids. You can be creative and add other things such as beans, rice, other veggies, or whatever meets your imagination. Makes 4 servings.

Cooking variation: You can make these at home using your kitchen oven. Prepare as directed above, place on a baking sheet, and cook at 325 degrees for 15–20 minutes.

You Wish It Were Chicken Legs

2 cups large chunks ham

2 cups large chunks veal

4 onions, quartered

Salt and pepper, to taste

$1/4$ cup milk or beaten egg

$1/2$ cup bread crumbs, crushed corn flakes, or cracker crumbs

$1/4$ cup water

Place chunks of ham and veal on skewer sticks, alternating with onion chunks. Salt and pepper, to taste. Roll in milk or egg and then in crumbs. Fry slowly over a low fire in a 12-inch cast iron skillet until the meat is brown, turning often. To make tender, pour water in the pan and simmer for 1 hour on very low heat, adding more water as needed. Excellent with greens or potatoes boiled with skins. Makes 4–6 servings.

Corn Soufflé

2 tablespoons dry bread crumbs

1 1/2 cups whole kernel corn

2 green onions, finely chopped

2 teaspoons vegetable oil

2/3 cup diced cooked ham

1/4 cup flour

1/4 teaspoon salt

1/8 teaspoon cayenne pepper

1 cup milk

1/2 cup grated cheddar cheese

4 eggs, room temperature

2 egg yolks

1/2 teaspoon cream of tartar

Preheat kitchen oven to 320 degrees or prepare 20 coals for cooking outside using a Dutch oven. Warm and grease a 10-inch Dutch oven and a 12-inch Dutch oven.

Lightly sprinkle bread crumbs in prepared 12-inch Dutch oven and set aside. In 10-inch Dutch oven, sauté the corn and onions in oil until tender. Stir in ham; remove mixture from Dutch oven, place in a bowl, and set aside.

In the 10-inch Dutch oven, combine flour, salt, and cayenne pepper. Gradually whisk in milk until smooth. Bring to a slow boil and cook until thickened. Remove from heat. Stir in cheese until melted. Add corn mixture. Let cool for 5 minutes, stirring occasionally.

Separate eggs; add the egg yolks plus the additional 2 yolks to the corn mixture gradually a little at a time so the yolks don't cook too fast. Allow to cool slightly. Meanwhile, in a large bowl, add cream of tartar to egg whites and beat until soft peaks form. With a spatula, fold a fourth of the egg whites into the corn mixture until no white streaks remain. Fold in remaining egg whites until combined. Pour mixture over bread crumbs in 12-inch Dutch oven. Bake for 50–55 minutes or until top is puffed and center appears set in your kitchen oven or use 8 coals on the bottom and 12 coals on the top of your Dutch oven. The smell will tell you when it's done. Makes 8 servings.

Dutch Oven Stuffed Onions

3 cups ground beef

1 cup sausage

3 eggs

2 cups bread crumbs, crushed corn flakes, cracker crumbs, or cooked rice

1 onion, finely chopped

1 cup celery, chopped

1 tablespoon all-purpose seasoning

1 cup stewed tomatoes, pureed, divided

1 green bell pepper, sliced in circles

2 large onions, halved and peeled in layers*(10–12 onion-section circles)

1/2 cup grated provolone, Monterey Jack, or Swiss cheese

Salt and pepper, to taste

Start 12 coals in a volcano or 25 coals in a charcoal starter. Grease a 12-inch Dutch oven.

Mix first 7 ingredients together in a large bowl. Add 1/2 cup of tomatoes and set aside. Place bell pepper slices around the bottom of the prepared Dutch oven. Place meat mixture inside of the onion sections and sit on top of pepper slices inside Dutch oven. Pour remaining 1/2 cup tomato mixture over onions and sprinkle lightly with salt and pepper.

Place Dutch oven in volcano on 12 coals and cook for 40 minutes with damper 1/2 open or place 10 coals under the Dutch oven in a circle and 15 on the top. When you get the smell, raise the lid, away from you, and sprinkle with cheese. Replace lid for 2–3 minutes and serve. Makes 10–12 servings.

Cooking variation: Using your kitchen oven, place Dutch oven on baking sheet and slide in a 300 degree oven for 40 minutes or until you can smell it.

*Run cold water on onion and layers will peel off easily. The inside of the leftover onion can be chopped and added to mixture.

Veggie Stuffed Peppers

1 medium onion, chopped

3 tablespoons butter, divided

1 medium tomato, chopped

1 (15-ounce) can whole kernel corn, drained

$1/2$ teaspoon salt

$1/2$ teaspoon dried basil

1 cup grated cheddar-jack cheese

1 cup fresh bread crumbs

3 large green bell peppers, cut in half lengthwise, stems and seeds removed

Preheat kitchen oven to 325 degrees or prepare 21 coals for cooking outside using a Dutch oven. Warm and grease a 10-inch Dutch oven.

In a large skillet, sauté onions in 2 tablespoons butter until tender. Add tomato, corn, salt, and basil. Cook until heated through, about 3–5 minutes. Stir in cheese and set aside. In a small bowl, combine bread crumbs and remaining butter.

Place peppers in prepared Dutch oven. Fill each pepper with about $1/2$ cup of vegetable mix. Sprinkle bread crumb mix evenly over the tops of all the peppers. Bake for 45–50 minutes in your kitchen oven or use 8 coals on the bottom and 13 coals on the top of your Dutch oven. Makes 6 servings.

Desserts

Cheese-and-Pumpkin Coffee Cake

1 yellow cake mix

1 (8-ounce) package cream cheese, softened

$^1/_2$ cup sour cream

$^3/_4$ cup canned pumpkin

6 tablespoons water

2 eggs

2 teaspoons pumpkin pie spice

1 teaspoon baking soda

1 teaspoon baking powder

Topping

$^1/_2$ cup chopped walnuts or pecans

$^1/_2$ cup packed brown sugar

$^1/_4$ cup flour

3 teaspoons butter, melted

Preheat kitchen oven to 325 degrees or prepare 25–26 coals for cooking outside using a Dutch oven. Warm and grease a 12-inch Dutch oven.

In a large bowl, combine the first 9 ingredients; mix well. In a small bowl, combine the topping ingredients.

Pour half of the pumpkin mixture into the prepared Dutch oven. Sprinkle half the topping mix on top of the pumpkin mix. Carefully spread the rest of the pumpkin mixture, followed by the rest of the topping mixture. Cover and bake for 35–40 minutes in your kitchen oven or use 10 coals on the bottom and 15–16 coals on the top of your Dutch oven. The smell of the spices will tell you when it is done. Makes 10–12 servings.

Cooking variation: This recipe can also be baked in a 9 x 13-inch cake pan. Metal or glass pans will work, but the taste from the cast iron can't be beat.

Apple Pie Cake

3 tablespoons shortening

1 cup sugar

1 egg

$1/2$ teaspoon cinnamon

$1/2$ teaspoon nutmeg

$1/2$ teaspoon salt

$1/2$ teaspoon baking powder

1 teaspoon baking soda

1 teaspoon vanilla

1 cup flour

3 cups peeled and diced apples

$1/2$ cup chopped walnuts or pecans

Preheat kitchen oven to 325 degrees. Warm and grease a 10-inch Dutch oven.

In a large bowl, combine shortening, sugar, and egg. Add spices and salt. Stir in baking powder, baking soda, and vanilla. Blend in flour, apples, and nuts. The mix will appear dry, but the moisture will come from the fresh apples. Spread in prepared Dutch oven and bake for 40–45 minutes. Serve warm or cold. Makes 8 servings.

Country Orange Wheat Cake

1 cup buttermilk

$3/4$ cup butter, softened

$1/4$ cup shortening

$2^1/2$ cups whole wheat flour

$1^1/2$ cups sugar

1 teaspoon baking soda

$1/2$ teaspoon baking powder

$3/4$ teaspoon salt

3 eggs

$1^1/2$ teaspoons vanilla

1 cup golden raisins

1 teaspoon grated orange peel

$1/4$ teaspoon orange flavoring

Frosting

$1/3$ cup butter, softened

3 cups powdered sugar

3 to 4 teaspoons orange juice

2 teaspoons grated orange peel

Preheat kitchen oven to 325 degrees. Grease and flour a 9 x 13-inch cake pan or warm and grease a 12-inch Dutch oven.

In a medium bowl, cream together first 3 ingredients and set aside. Combine the dry ingredients in a large bowl and stir in the buttermilk mixture. Add the remaining ingredients and mix well to combine the flavors. Pour batter into prepared pan and bake for 45 minutes.

While cake is baking, cream all frosting ingredients together in a large bowl and then chill. Let the cake cool for 20 minutes. Frost the cake and serve. Makes 12–16 servings.

Cooking variation: Prepare 25–26 coals for cooking outside using a 12-inch Dutch oven. Follow above instructions and bake for 45 minutes using 10 coals on the bottom and 15–16 coals on top of your Dutch oven.

Chocolate Idaho Bean Cake

2 cups mashed pinto or red beans

2 eggs

$1/4$ cup butter, softened

1 cup sugar

$1/4$ teaspoon salt

1 teaspoon baking soda

$1\,1/2$ teaspoons vanilla

1 teaspoon cinnamon

$1/4$ teaspoon nutmeg

$1/4$ teaspoon ground cloves

1 cup flour

2 cups diced apples or 1 (29-ounce) can apple pie filling

$3/4$ cup raisins, optional

$1/2$ cup chocolate chips or 4 tablespoons cocoa, optional

$1/4$ cup chopped nuts

Preheat kitchen oven to 325 degrees or prepare 25–27 coals for cooking outside using a Dutch oven. Warm and grease a 12-inch Dutch oven.

In a large bowl, cream together the beans, eggs, butter, and sugar. Add salt, baking soda, vanilla, and spices. Stir in flour and blend well. Fold in apples, raisins, and chocolate. Pour into prepared Dutch oven and sprinkle the nuts on top.

Bake for about 35–40 minutes in your kitchen over or use 10–12 coals on the bottom and 15 coals on the top of your Dutch oven. The smell will tell you when it's done. Makes 10–12 servings.

Mama Belle's Moist Chocolate Cake

1 cup buttermilk or sour milk

1 teaspoon vanilla

$1/2$ teaspoon salt

2 teaspoons baking soda

2 cups flour

$1/2$ teaspoon baking powder

$1/2$ cup cocoa

2 eggs

1 cup hot water

Preheat kitchen oven to 300 degrees or prepare 24–26 coals for cooking outside using a Dutch oven. Warm and grease a 12-inch Dutch oven.

Mix all ingredients together except water in prepared Dutch oven. When all dry ingredients are moistened, slowly pour in hot water. Continue to mix until batter is very runny. Bake for about 35 minutes in your kitchen oven or use 9–10 coals on the bottom and 15–16 coals on the top of your Dutch oven. The smell of the cake will tell you when it's done. Served warm with ice cream on top is the best. Makes 10–12 servings.

Cooking variation: You can also bake this cake in a 9 x 13-inch glass or metal pan.

Lemon "Oh My Gosh" Pudding Cake

1 cup sugar

$1/4$ teaspoon salt

2 teaspoons grated lemon rind

3 tablespoons lemon juice

$1/2$ teaspoon orange flavoring

3 eggs

$1/3$ cup flour

2 tablespoons butter, melted

$1\,1/2$ cups milk

Preheat kitchen oven to 325 degrees or prepare 24 coals for cooking outside using a Dutch oven. Grease a 10-inch Dutch oven.

In a large bowl, mix sugar, salt, lemon rind, lemon juice, orange flavoring, and eggs together. Beat well and add flour. Blend in butter and milk. Pour into prepared Dutch oven. Cover and bake for 40–50 minutes in your kitchen oven or use 9 coals on the bottom and 15 coals on the top of your Dutch oven. The smell of the lemon and orange will tell you it's done. Makes 8 servings.

TIP: When you bake in your kitchen oven using a Dutch oven, put the lid on to keep the moisture inside.

Marmalade Pound Cake

1 white cake mix

1 (3.4-ounce) box instant vanilla pudding mix

$^1/_2$ cup sour cream

$^1/_3$ cup butter, softened

$^1/_2$ cup orange juice

1 tablespoon grated orange peel

3 eggs

$^1/_2$ cup apricot or orange marmalade

1 cup chopped walnuts or pecans

Glaze

1 cup powdered sugar

1 tablespoon milk

1 tablespoon orange juice

$^1/_2$ teaspoon grated orange peel

Preheat kitchen oven to 325 degrees or prepare 24–25 coals for cooking outside using a Dutch oven. Warm, grease, and flour a 12-inch Dutch oven.

In a large bowl, combine cake mix, pudding mix, sour cream, butter, orange juice, orange peel, and eggs; mix thoroughly. Fold in marmalade and nuts. Pour batter prepared Dutch oven. Cover and bake for 50–60 minutes in your kitchen oven or use 9 coals on the bottom and 15–16 coals on the top of your Dutch oven. The cake is done when golden brown and a toothpick inserted in center comes out clean. Cool for 10 minutes in the Dutch oven. Invert onto serving plate and allow to cool completely.

In a small bowl, combine glaze ingredients until smooth. Drizzle over cooled cake. Makes 10–12 servings.

My Favorite Pineapple-Carrot Cake

1 1/2 cups vegetable oil

2 cups sugar

3 cups flour

1 1/2 teaspoons baking soda

1/2 teaspoon baking powder

3 teaspoons cinnamon

1/4 teaspoon nutmeg

2 carrots, grated

1 (20-ounce) can crushed pineapple

1/2 cup chopped walnuts

3 eggs

2 teaspoons vanilla

Preheat kitchen oven to 300 degrees or prepare 24–26 coals for cooking outside using a Dutch oven. Warm and grease a 12-inch Dutch oven.

In a large bowl, mix oil and sugar together and set aside. Combine dry ingredients in a medium bowl and add half of the dry mixture to the sugar mixture. Mix well and beat in carrots, pineapple, and nuts. Add eggs, one at a time, and beat until well blended. Add the vanilla and the rest of dry ingredients and mix well.

Pour the batter into the prepared Dutch oven. Cover and bake for about 35–40 minutes in your kitchen oven or use 9–10 coals on the bottom and 15–16 coals on the top of your Dutch oven. Makes 20–24 servings.

Variation: A cream cheese frosting is tasty on this cake. Mix together 1 (8-ounce) package of cream cheese and 2 cups of powdered sugar with 2 tablespoons of milk to make a creamy frosting. Sprinkle the top with nuts. You can also just sprinkle the top of the cake with cinnamon and sugar.

Peanut Butter Cake

1/2 cup smooth peanut butter

1/2 cup shortening

2 1/2 cups sifted cake flour

2 teaspoons baking powder

1/2 teaspoon baking soda

1 teaspoon salt

1/2 teaspoon cinnamon

1/4 teaspoon allspice

1 1/2 cups sugar

3/4 cup milk

2 eggs

1 teaspoon vanilla

Frosting

1 (16–ounce) container milk chocolate frosting

1 tablespoon grated orange peel

1 cup chopped roasted peanuts

Preheat kitchen oven to 325 degrees or prepare 24 coals for cooking outside using a Dutch oven. Warm, grease, and lightly flour a 12-inch Dutch oven.

In a large bowl, beat together the peanut butter and shortening; set aside. Sift together the cake flour, baking powder, baking soda, salt, cinnamon, allspice, and sugar in a separate large bowl. Add the dry ingredients and milk to the peanut butter mixture. Mix well and add eggs and vanilla. Beat 1 minute more.

Pour the batter into the prepared Dutch oven. Cover and bake for 45 minutes in your kitchen oven or use 9 coals on the bottom and 15 coals on the top of your Dutch oven. Waiting for the smell is the best way to know it's done. Remove the cake from Dutch oven and cool completely before frosting.

In a medium bowl, combine the frosting ingredients and frost the cooled cake. Makes 14–16 servings.

Cooking variation: You can also grease and flour a 9 x 13-inch baking pan and bake for 45 minutes.

Praline Rum Cake

1 cup finely chopped pecans

1 white cake mix

1 (3.4-ounce) box instant vanilla pudding mix

4 eggs

³/4 cup cold water, divided

¹/4 cup vegetable oil

¹/2 cup dark rum, divided

1 cup sugar

¹/2 cup butter

¹/2 cup water

Sliced peaches

Whipped topping

Preheat kitchen oven to 325 degrees. Grease and flour a 10-inch Dutch oven or grease and flour a 9 x 13-inch cake pan.

Sprinkle the pecans evenly in bottom of prepared pan of choice. In a large bowl, combine cake mix, pudding mix, eggs, ¹/4 cup water, oil, and ¹/4 cup rum. Beat for 2 minutes to blend well. Pour over pecans. Bake for 50–55 minutes or until cake tests done. The smell will tell you when to peek at your cake. Cool in pan for 15 minutes. Invert on serving plate.

In small saucepan, combine sugar, butter, and remaining water. Boil for 5 minutes, stirring constantly. This can be done while cake is cooling. Remove from heat. Stir in remaining rum until heated through. Spoon hot glaze over warm cake. Serve with peaches and whipped topping, or ice cream, if desired. This is a very sweet cake. Makes 12–14 servings.

Utah Pound Cake

3/4 **cup butter**

1 1/2 **cups sugar**

3 **eggs**

1 **teaspoon vanilla**

1/4 **teaspoon almond or lemon extract**

2 1/3 **cups flour, unsifted**

1/2 **teaspoon baking powder**

1/2 **teaspoon salt**

1/2 **teaspoon cinnamon**

1/2 **teaspoon nutmeg**

3/4 **cup milk**

Preheat kitchen oven to 325 degrees or prepare 25 coals for cooking outside using a Dutch oven. Grease and flour a 9 x 13-inch cake pan or a 12-inch Dutch oven.

In a large bowl, beat butter and sugar until light and fluffy. Add eggs and beat well again. Add the flavorings. In a medium bowl, blend dry ingredients together and then add to butter mixture alternating with the milk; mix well. Pour batter into prepared pan or Dutch oven. Bake for 1 hour in your kitchen oven or use 10 coals on the bottom and 15 coals on the top of your Dutch oven. The cake is done when the top springs back when lightly touched.

Cool in pan or Dutch oven on rack for 15 minutes. Remove from Dutch oven by turning upside down on the lid. Cool and serve with whipped cream or ice cream. Makes 12–14 servings.

Strawberry Shortcakes

2 cups Bisquick mix

2 tablespoons sugar

$1/2$ cup butter

$1/2$ cup milk

Fresh or frozen strawberries, sweetened

Sweetened whipped cream

Preheat kitchen oven to 425 degrees or prepare 26–27 coals for cooking outside using a Dutch oven. Warm and lightly grease a baking sheet or a 12-inch Dutch oven.

In a large bowl, combine Bisquick mix and sugar. Stir or cut in butter until mixture resembles coarse crumbs. Add milk. Stir only until the mixture is dampened. Pour out on a lightly floured board and knead gently for a few seconds. Roll or pat dough to half inch thick. Cut in circles. Place shortcakes on prepared baking sheet or in Dutch oven and bake for about 10–12 minutes in your kitchen oven or use 9 coals on the bottom and 17–18 on the top of your Dutch oven.

Split the shortcakes while warm. Spoon strawberries between halves and top with whipped cream. Makes 12 servings.

Variation: Bananas can be substituted for strawberries or mixed together.

Cherry-Chocolate Surprise

1 (29-ounce) can cherry pie filling

1 cup coconut

$^1/_2$ cup slivered almonds

1 box devil's food or red velvet cake mix

$^2/_3$ (12-ounce) can Coke

Preheat kitchen oven to 325 degrees or prepare 20 coals for cooking outside using a Dutch oven. Warm and grease a 10-inch Dutch oven.

Combine pie filling, coconut, and almonds in prepared Dutch oven. Sprinkle cake mix over the filling. Drizzle Coke over cake mix. Bake for about 30 minutes in your kitchen oven or use 8 coals on the bottom and 12 coals on the top of your Dutch oven. The smell will alert you when it's ready. Top with whipped cream. Makes 8–10 servings.

Cowgirl Apple Pie Cake

4 cups thinly sliced apples

$1/4$ cup packed brown sugar

$1\,1/2$ teaspoons apple pie spice

$1/2$ cup chopped walnuts

1 cup flour

$1/2$ cup butter, softened

$3/4$ teaspoon baking powder

$1/3$ cup heavy cream

$3/4$ cup sugar

3 tablespoons water

$3/4$ cup sugar

1 egg

Cinnamon sugar (1 teaspoon cinnamon mixed with $1/4$ cup sugar)

Preheat kitchen oven to 325 degrees or prepare 25 coals for cooking outside using a Dutch oven. Warm and grease a 10-inch Dutch oven.

Place the apples in the bottom of prepared Dutch oven. Sprinkle with brown sugar, spice, and walnuts.

In a large bowl, combine the remaining ingredients to make a thick batter. Pour over the apple mixture. Sprinkle with cinnamon sugar. Bake for about 1 hour in your kitchen oven or use 10 coals on the bottom and 15 coals on the top of your Dutch oven. The smell will tell you when it is done. Makes 8–10 servings.

Whipped Peanut Butter Pie

1 (2-ounce) envelope unflavored gelatin

$1/2$ cup sugar, divided

$1/4$ teaspoon salt

1 cup evaporated milk

2 egg yolks, slightly beaten

$2/3$ cup creamy peanut butter

2 egg whites

1 (4.5-ounce) container whipped topping

1 (9-inch) graham cracker crumb pie shell

Caramel or chocolate syrup

Combine gelatin, $1/4$ cup sugar, and salt in a medium saucepan. Stir in milk and egg yolks. Cook and stir over medium heat until mixture comes to a boil. Remove from heat; add peanut butter, stirring until smooth. Chill, stirring occasionally, until mixture thickens and is partially set.

In a large bowl, beat egg whites until foamy. Gradually beat in remaining $1/4$ cup sugar and continue beating until mixture forms stiff, shiny peaks. Fold in peanut butter mixture and then fold in whipped topping. Spoon into shell. Chill until firm, about 2 hours. Drizzle top with syrup. Makes 8 servings.

Fruity Cobbler

1 (29-ounce) can fruit or pie filling

1 cake mix

$2/3$ can of cream soda, Sprite, Coke, root beer, or soda pop of choice

Sprinkle of cinnamon or nutmeg or both

Preheat kitchen oven to 325 degrees or prepare 25 coals for cooking outside using a Dutch oven. Warm and grease a 12-inch Dutch oven.

Pour fruit or filling into prepared Dutch oven and spread over bottom. Pour cake mix into Dutch oven and stir into fruit. Add as much soda pop as needed to give moisture. Sprinkle with cinnamon or nutmeg. Cover and bake for 20–35 minutes in your kitchen oven or use 10 coals on the bottom and 15 coals on the top of your Dutch oven. Wait for the smell; it's the best way to know it's done. Top with ice cream or whipped topping. Makes 10–12 servings.

Possible combinations of cake mixes and fruits

Yellow cake mix with peaches, drain juice

Spice cake mix with apple pie filling

White or yellow cake mix with blueberry pie filling

Yellow cake mix with cherry pie filling

Lemon cake mix with pineapple or bananas

Yellow cake mix with fruit cocktail or mandarin oranges, drain juice

Chocolate cake mix with cherry pie filling

Spice cake mix with pumpkin and apple

White cake mix with raspberries

There are limitless combinations. Make up a few of your own and have fun.

Dutch Oven Pumpkin-Apple Cobbler

1 (15-ounce) can pumpkin pie filling

1 (15-ounce) can apple pie filling

1 box spice cake mix

$^1/_2$ cup crumbled Nilla Wafers or Pecan Sandies

$^1/_2$ cup chopped pecans

$^2/_3$ can of 7UP or root beer

Cinnamon and nutmeg or apple pie spice

Preheat kitchen oven to 300 degrees or prepare 25 coals for cooking outside using a Dutch oven. Warm a 12-inch Dutch oven and lightly coat with grease.

Empty both cans of pie filling in bottom of oven and lightly mix. Sprinkle cake mix over the top. Sprinkle crumbled cookies and nuts over the mixture and drizzle 7UP over the top. Sprinkle with a little nutmeg and cinnamon. Bake for 35 minutes in your kitchen oven or use 10 coals on the bottom and 15 coals on the top of your Dutch oven. Cook until you can smell the cobbler and steam seeps out from under the lid. Serve with ice cream or whipped cream. Makes 10–12 servings.

Apple Fritters

2 cups vegetable oil

1 cup evaporated milk

2 eggs, beaten

2 cups flour

1 teaspoon baking powder

Pinch of salt

4 tart apples, peeled, cored, and thinly sliced

Preheat oil in a large cast iron skillet to approximately 400 degrees.

In a medium saucepan, heat the milk to a little more than lukewarm; slowly add in the eggs, flour, baking powder, and salt. Throw in slices of apples, dipping the batter over them. Drop by spoonfuls into hot oil, fry to a golden brown, and serve with maple syrup or a caramel topping. Makes approximately 16 servings.

Variation: For a tasty treat, roll the cooked fritters in cinnamon and sugar or powdered sugar.

Carrot Pudding

¹/₂ cup butter

1 cup packed brown sugar

2 eggs, beaten

1 cup grated carrots

1 cup grated apples

1 cup raisins

2 cups bread crumbs

¹/₂ cup flour

2 teaspoons baking powder

¹/₄ teaspoon baking soda

¹/₂ teaspoon salt

1 teaspoon cinnamon

1 teaspoon nutmeg

¹/₂ teaspoon ground cloves

Preheat kitchen oven to 300 degrees or prepare 42 coals for cooking outside using a Dutch oven. Warm and grease a 12-inch Dutch oven.

In a large bowl, whip the butter and gradually add in the brown sugar. Add in the eggs, carrots, raisins, and apples. Add the dry ingredients and combine. Pour into prepared Dutch oven, filling 2/3 full and cover. Bake for 2 hours in your kitchen oven or use 8 coals on the bottom and 13 coals on the top of your Dutch oven. You will need to replace the coals after the first hour of cooking. Bake low and slow, the smell will tell you when it's done. Makes 12 servings.

Crispy Popcorn

1 cup sugar

$1/2$ cup butter

$1/2$ cup dark corn syrup

$1/2$ teaspoon salt

3 or more quarts popped popcorn

Preheat kitchen oven to 300 degrees.

In medium saucepan, boil the first 4 ingredients for about 4 minutes. This will be at a medium ball stage when dropped in a glass of cold water. Pour over popped corn in shallow pan and place in oven. Bake for 30 minutes, stirring often. Let cool for 30 minutes. This will be similar to making popcorn balls but you will break it in pieces like cracker jacks when cooled. Makes 3 quarts popcorn.

Delicious Snowballs

- $1/2$ **cup butter**
- **1 egg yolk**
- $1/2$ **cup sugar**
- $3/4$ **cup chopped walnuts or pecans**
- **1 (20-ounce) can crushed pineapple, drained**
- **1 (12-ounce) box vanilla wafers**
- **1 pint whipping cream**
- $1/4$ **teaspoon vanilla**
- **1 cup shredded coconut**

In a large bowl, cream together the butter, egg yolk, and sugar. Add nuts and pineapple. Stir until well blended. Spread mixture between 3 wafers to make it like a ball. Whip cream with vanilla until it forms soft peaks. Spread cream around snowball and roll in coconut. Place on a baking sheet and freeze overnight. Take out of freezer 2–3 hours before serving. You can garnish with cherries, blueberries, strawberries, or eat plain. Makes 12–15 snowballs.

Butterfinger Balls

1 pound powdered sugar

$1/2$ cup butter, softened

1 cup creamy peanut butter

3 cups Rice Krispies

16 ounces melted milk chocolate

1 cup chopped pecans or walnuts

In a large bowl, mix all of the ingredients together by hand. Shape into balls and place on a baking sheet. Chill at least 1 hour. Dip each ball into melted chocolate and roll in chopped nuts. Makes about 20–24 balls.

Brown Sugar Candy Roll

$1/4$ cup water

$1/3$ cup light Karo syrup

1 pound brown sugar

1 cup sugar

$1 1/2$ cups heavy cream

4 tablespoons butter

1 teaspoon vanilla

1 cup finely chopped nuts, divided

Combine the first 6 ingredients together in a 10-inch Dutch oven. Cook to soft ball stage when tested in a small glass of cold water. Cool and beat until the mixture thickens. Add vanilla and $1/2$ of the nuts. Mix in thoroughly. The mix will continue to thicken. Mold into rolls and roll the filling in the remaining nuts. Makes 3 or more rolls.

Quick No-Bake Haystacks

1 cup butterscotch chips

$^1/_2$ cup white chocolate chips

$^1/_2$ cup creamy peanut butter

1 cup miniature marshmallows

$^1/_2$ cup peanuts or cashew pieces

2 cups chow mein noodles

In a large microwave-safe bowl, melt chips and peanut butter together in microwave. Fold in marshmallows, peanuts, and chow mein noodles. Drop by teaspoonfuls onto waxed paper. Cool until set. Makes 30–36 pieces.

Nutty Peanut Clusters

2 cups sugar

1 cup packed brown sugar

2 tablespoons light corn syrup

1 $^1/_2$ cups water

$^1/_4$ teaspoon salt

1 teaspoon vanilla

2 cups nuts, raw peanuts, walnuts, pecans, almonds, or a mix of all kinds, whole or chopped

In a large bowl, combine sugars, syrup, water, and salt. Cook over low heat until soft ball forms in cold water. Remove from heat, add vanilla and nuts, stir for about 1 minute. Drop by teaspoonfuls on wax paper. Makes 24–30 clusters.

Penuche

2 cups packed brown sugar

1 cup sugar

1 cup evaporated milk

$^1/_3$ cup white corn syrup

2 tablespoons butter

$^1/_4$ teaspoon salt

1 teaspoon vanilla

1 cup chopped walnuts or pecans

In a large saucepan, boil all ingredients together except the vanilla and nuts until mixture reaches soft ball stage. Do not stir. Pour out onto greased platter or baking sheet with sides, add vanilla then cool.

When cool, beat until it is thick enough to mold into teaspoon-size rolls. After molding into rolls, cover with chopped nuts. Makes about 24–30 rolls.

Pecan Chocolate Drops

2 1/4 cups packed brown sugar

1 cup butter

1 cup light corn syrup

1/8 teaspoon salt

1 (14-ounce) can sweetened condensed milk

1 teaspoon vanilla

1 pound pecan pieces

2 (1-ounce) squares white chocolate

2 tablespoons shortening

Combine sugar, butter, corn syrup, and salt in a 10-inch Dutch oven. Cook over medium heat until sugar is dissolved. Gradually add the milk and mix well. Heat until the candy thermometer reads 248 degrees or hard ball stage. Remove from heat and stir in vanilla. Fold in pecans. Drop by tablespoonfuls onto a wax paper lined baking sheet. Chill until firm.

Melt chocolate and shortening in a double boiler or microwave and drizzle chocolate over each cluster. This is a fun candy to make and you can substitute dark chocolate for white. Makes 24–30 drops.

Pumpkin Fudge

1 cup milk

3 cups sugar

$^2/_3$ cup pumpkin pie filling

4 tablespoons light corn syrup

$^1/_4$ teaspoon salt

$^1/_4$ cup butter, softened

1 teaspoon pumpkin pie spice

$^1/_2$ cup chopped nuts

1 $^1/_2$ teaspoons vanilla

In a large saucepan, combine milk, sugar, pumpkin, syrup, and salt and mix thoroughly. Over medium heat, bring mixture to a bubbly boil, stirring constantly. Reduce heat to low medium, and continue boiling mixture without stirring until it reaches the soft ball stage when dropped into cold water, which is 232 degrees on a candy thermometer.

Remove saucepan from heat and stir in butter, pumpkin pie spice, nuts, and vanilla. Let fudge cool to lukewarm (about 100 degrees), then beat mixture until it becomes very thick and loses some of its gloss. Pour fudge into a buttered 8 x 8-inch pan. When firm, cut into squares. Makes 15–24 servings.

Variation: For thinner pieces, use a 9 x 13-inch pan.

Index

172

173

Colleen Sloan

Raised on a farm near Promontory Summit, Utah, Colleen has been an outdoor gal from the moment she was born. Working and living in the outdoors is part of her heritage. Her grandparents came west as pioneers using hand carts and covered wagons and her addiction to cooking with Dutch ovens started at an early age. Her mother cooked many a meal in the farmhouse on a coal and wood stove. Her mother was an excellent cook. With that heritage, a handwritten cookbook of old pioneer recipes, a father who was a Scoutmaster for 38 years, her own 45 years in Scouting, county fairs, and 4H, you can see how her career as an outdoor expert and master Dutch oven chef came to be. Her grandmother is quoted as saying "it is the healthiest kind of cookin' we can do for our families."

Colleen loves to share knowledge and swap recipes with other Dutch oven fans and in that pursuit, teaches at the College of Southern Idaho and gives seminars at sports shows throughout the United States. In her spare time, her love of the outdoors continues as she fishes, camps, and hunts with her children, grandchildren, and great-grandchildren. Colleen is the author of 7 books, loves to teach Dutch oven cooking, and, with her history, good stories, and funny antidotes, brings warmth and laughter to each of her seminars. Like her grandma and mom used to say, "Kissin' wears out, but cookin', don't."

Metric Conversion Chart

Volume Measurements		Weight Measurements		Temperature Conversion	
U.S.	Metric	U.S.	Metric	Fahrenheit	Celsius
1 teaspoon	5 ml	1/2 ounce	15 g	250	120
1 tablespoon	15 ml	1 ounce	30 g	300	150
1/4 cup	60 ml	3 ounces	90 g	325	160
1/3 cup	75 ml	4 ounces	115 g	350	180
1/2 cup	125 ml	8 ounces	225 g	375	190
2/3 cup	150 ml	12 ounces	350 g	400	200
3/4 cup	175 ml	1 pound	450 g	425	220
1 cup	250 ml	2 1/4 pounds	1 kg	450	230